Thanks are due to *Admap*, where the articles in their original form were first published, and to WARC, who retains copyright to them as published in their original form

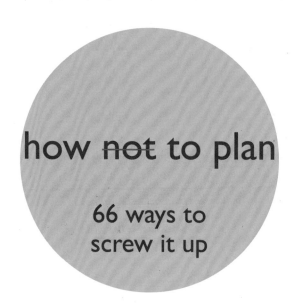

how ~~not~~ to plan

66 ways to
screw it up

by

Les Binet & Sarah Carter

Matador
9 Priory Business Park,
Wistow Road, Kibworth Beauchamp,
Leicestershire. LE8 0RX
Tel: 0116 279 2299
Email: books@troubador.co.uk
Web: www.troubador.co.uk/matador
Twitter: @matadorbooks

ISBN 978 1789014 501

British Library Cataloguing in Publication Data.
A catalogue record for this book is available from the British Library.

Printed and bound by CPI Group (UK) Ltd, Croydon, CR0 4YY
Typeset in 11pt Gill Sans by Troubador Publishing Ltd, Leicester, UK

Matador is an imprint of Troubador Publishing Ltd

Les and Sarah have debated, laughed, despaired and generally
tried to get better at planning together for more than 30 years at
12 Bishops Bridge Road, London.

During this time, they've written more than
50 award-winning IPA Advertising Effectiveness papers, and been privileged
to work alongside the best planners in the world.

This book is dedicated to you all.
We stand on the shoulders of giants.

'Always read something that will make you look good if you die in the middle of it'

PJ O'Rourke

FOREWORD

Planning is now over 50 years old, and it's more diverse, more interesting and practised by more people than ever; so it's timely that the APG should publish this excellent book by Les Binet and Sarah Carter.

Those of you who have been around for some, or even all, of the APG's own life will be familiar with previous volumes published by the APG: the original 'Blue Book', called *How to Plan Advertising*, and its younger sibling, the 'Red Book', which for many years served as excellent reference and guidance.

Everything in our professional world moves so fast that we might now hesitate to publish an authoritative volume on the craft and practice of planning for fear of speedy obsolescence. But despite changing circumstances, there are eternal principles and rules, and ways of approaching problems that remain helpful – and we're keen to uphold them. We think they will continue to guide planners, strategists, marketers and researchers for many years to come. And it is these principles and ideas that Les and Sarah have used to create this incisive 'How To', or rather, 'How Not To'.

The eagle-eyed among you will already have observed the contrarian title. We like a bit of contrary thinking, but there is nothing irrelevant or out of place about the contents of this book. It's meticulously researched and incredibly detailed about what to do, and what not to do, at the different stages of the planning process. It's written with a lightness of touch and a sense of humour, and embellished with lots of relevant and interesting examples and charts.

We've designed the book with practicality in mind. You should be able to shove it in your bag and take it to a meeting, scrawl in your own ideas, make notes in it, and enjoy having it next to you on your desk.

So, for all of you, here's your book. Enjoy it, savour it – and use it.

Sarah Newman
Director, APG

INTRODUCTION

To be honest, we're not big fans of 'business books'. Like you, no doubt, we have shelves full of them. Most we've not finished. Many we've not even started. None are actually *used*.

So, we'd like this book to be different.

We don't want it to be clever. We just hope that it's *useful* – on your desk, coffee-stained and well-thumbed.

This is not the complete 'how to do it' manual of planning – if ever there could be such a thing. Instead, it all started back in 2010 with a series of monthly articles we began writing for *Admap*. These were all loosely based on a myth-busting theme. But really, they were just a welcome outlet to vent our frustration at the bollocks we kept encountering on the planning frontline.

We thought we might run to a couple of years' worth of articles. Six years later, we were still going strong…

As an industry, we celebrate and share the good stuff. Meanwhile, the 'less said about that the better' stuff is swept out of sight… for obvious reasons. But through writing these articles, we came to realise that we perhaps learn more from the myths, misunderstandings and screw-ups than from the successes. And so our articles started to become useful little summaries to answer questions from planners. And planners, in turn, found them good jumping-off points for client discussions on similar real-life issues.

So now with permission from *Admap*, and support from the APG, we've collated all 66 'how not to do it' articles here. We've grouped them into nine chapters around the planning cycle. And we've added extra material: checklists, mini case studies, tools, charts and observations.

This is the little book we'd have liked on *our* desks when we started out some 30 years ago.

Hope it's useful.

Les and Sarah
adam&eveDDB

FINDING YOUR WAY AROUND

1 SETTING OBJECTIVES

2 PRODUCT, PRICE AND PLACE

3 BRAND AND COMMUNICATION

4 RESEARCH AND ANALYSIS

5 TALKING AND THINKING ABOUT STRATEGY

6 WHO ARE YOU TALKING TO?

7 BUDGETS AND MEDIA

8 CREATIVE WORK

9 EFFECTIVENESS AND EVALUATION

Notes:

_____

_____

_____

_____

_____

_____

_____

_____

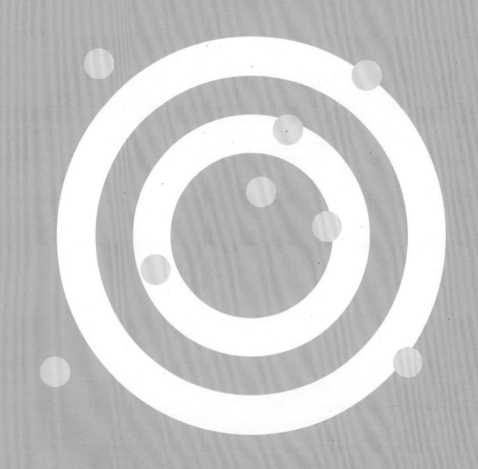

SETTING
OBJECTIVES

'If you don't know where you are going, any road will take you there'

Lewis Carroll

ONE

INTRODUCTION

Effective communication starts with agreeing with your clients what it's supposed to do.

This sounds simple. But so often, this stage is rushed, fudged, based on flawed thinking or skipped altogether. And then the consequences come back to bite us… How can we pre-test this ad if we've never agreed what it's meant to do? How do we measure effectiveness if the available research can't measure what the advertising was planned to do? Was 'failure' a result of advertising being flawed? Or did we just not spend enough money for enough people to see it?

In this first chapter, we look at how to get off to the right start; how to set sensible objectives; how to think through what your communication can do; and how it might realistically do this.

Should we focus on existing customers or new ones? Do we want more buying or more buyers? How much do we need to worry about alienating the buyers we have as we try to appeal to new ones?

All based on empirical knowledge and hard-earned experience, rather than wishful thinking, received wisdom or guesswork.

HOW ~~NOT~~ TO MAKE A PLAN

'A goal without a plan is just a wish'
Antoine de Saint-Exupéry

We once received a brief for a famous brand that had lost its way. The brief stated the brand ambition as being to 'Take the brand back to greatness'. Then it set an objective of adding 13 percentage points of penetration, and increasing brand share back to levels not seen for a decade.

All very ambitious. But nowhere in the rest of the brief was there anything about how to achieve these heady objectives. No radical new positioning. No new audience or usage occasion identified. No new channel thinking. And no increase in budget. In short, a total disconnect existed between objectives and plans – or more accurately, between marketing fantasy and reality.

This is something we seem to be coming across more nowadays: marketing objectives that have lost their grip on reality. Interestingly, the bigger the client, the worse this syndrome appears to be.

We don't know why. Perhaps it reflects more pressure in global companies to deliver impressive numbers. Or a greater distance between global management and the practical realities of delivering those results.

Management consultants tell us that objectives should always be 'SMART': Specific, Measurable, Achievable, Realistic and Timed. In our experience, they rarely are.

It's amazing how often clients happily commit huge sums of money with no clear objectives. Even when objectives *are* specified, they're often incredibly vague. One company recently spent millions of pounds without defining their objectives any more clearly than to 'sell a shedload of X'.

Or, there might be defined objectives, but they're totally unrealistic. It's actually very rare for brands to make big gains in market share, penetration or anything else. Yet, when did you last see a brand plan not stating this as an aim?

Macho marketing language is common, but dangerous. And objective setting is where it's perhaps most dangerous. Marketing plans are littered with words like 'disrupting' and 'transforming'. Plans hardly ever use more modest, but more realistic, words like 'nudging', 'reinforcing' or 'reassuring' – they just don't sound impressive enough. It probably doesn't help that the box on the brief titled 'objective' has often been replaced nowadays by one called 'ambition' or 'vision'. And when the brand plan writer won't be there in two years' time anyway, they may as well write wishful bullshit.

But why does all this matter?

Well, because there is evidence from the IPA Databank that better objective setting leads to more effective campaigns. Best practice is to identify exactly what business results you want. And exactly what you need people to think, feel and do in order to deliver those results.

The Databank also reminds us that reach and 'Share of Voice' (SOV) are crucial. No matter how well thought through your objectives, or how good your creative work, a campaign can't deliver unless it reaches enough people. It's also unlikely to succeed if it doesn't outshout the competition. These are basic hygiene factors, but too often ignored by the wishful thinkers of marketing.

So let's stop dreaming. By all means let's be ambitious. But root your ambitions in knowledge and reality. Remember: 'A goal without a plan is just a wish'.

HOW TO MAKE A PLAN

2 minute checklist

o   Set and agree clear objectives.
    Are they 'SMART'?

o   Start with business objectives: targets for sales, profit,
    market share etc.

o   Then set marketing objectives: customer numbers, weight
    of purchase, distribution etc.

o   Crunch the numbers. Even back-of-an-envelope stuff helps.
    Can your marketing objectives realistically deliver the business
    objectives?

o   Think people, not just numbers. Who do you need to influence?
    What do you want them to do, exactly? Instead of what?

o   If necessary, commission extra research. Simple omnibus questions
    can often be enough.

o   Only then set communications objectives. Who are your audience?
    How can you influence them?

o   Check your budgets. Can you reach enough people? What will
    your SOV be?

o   Set 'Key Performance Indicators' (KPIs) for each objective,
    and start tracking them.

o   Evaluate your results against those KPIs.

HOW TO MAKE A PLAN
JOHN LEWIS

Useful case study

The 2016 John Lewis IPA case is a good example of how to set objectives. John Lewis's ultimate aim is to keep its 'Partners' (permanent employees) happy. The paper shows how this informed the company's plan, from business/commercial objectives through marketing objectives to communications goals. The KPIs by which success would be measured then flowed from the plan.

Objectives of John Lewis Christmas advertising

HOW ~~NOT~~ TO DEFINE YOUR COMPETITION

'Your customers are the customers of other brands
who occasionally buy you'
Andrew Ehrenberg

A couple of years ago, we reviewed an ice cream brand. It had dominated its category for decades, but had recently lost the top spot to a similar rival. What had gone wrong?

We soon noticed something. Our brand had lost market share to its doppelgänger. But more interestingly, *both* brands had been losing market share for years to a host of smaller competitors. These together now accounted for a bigger market share than either 'market leader'.

Further analysis suggested why. The two big brands had followed identical marketing strategies. In trying to increase 'Return on Investment' (ROI) and efficiency, each reduced marketing expenditure. Each cut emotional brand

advertising in favour of 'harder selling' stuff focused on 'new news'. Each replaced expensive broadcast media with cheaper digital channels; this tighter targeting allowing both brands to reduce 'wastage'.

But without big, famous advertising, the public started to forget about these two brand leaders. And when they did think about them, they felt less warm towards them. So despite product improvements, ratings deteriorated and people started experimenting with alternatives.

Surprisingly, our brand's marketing team hadn't noticed. They were so focused on their immediate rival they failed to spot the little brands stealing their customers; the other brand probably suffered from the same blinkered view.

We've seen this happen before. Adam Morgan even has a name for it: the 'Mephisto Waltz'. Two big brands become so obsessed with competing against each other that they become mirror images: each copying the other's strategy, each benchmarking itself against the other – making it easy for challenger brands to sneak in and grab share. If the market leaders don't notice in time, then the Mephisto Waltz becomes a death spiral.

How does this happen? Why don't brands realise what's going on? There are three main reasons.

First, a focus on efficiency, not on effectiveness. Big brands with high market share find it hard to increase revenue. So they focus on cost cutting. Our brand was just focused on short-term ROI. Its competitor had the same obsession. But cutting their budgets destroyed the foundations of their success.

When marketing efficiency is the focus, targeting and segmentation come to the fore. And that's the second problem. Like many marketers, our clients focused on a tightly defined market segment. When shown how customers were defecting to the smaller brands, they argued that these weren't competitors. Some were too cheap. Others too premium. They defined their market segment so narrowly, there was only one other brand in it: their big rival.

But as Andrew Ehrenberg and Byron Sharp have shown, markets are much less segmented than people think. We all use a repertoire of brands – Waitrose shoppers pop into Lidl too – so all category brands compete with one another to some extent.

The third problem is short-termism. When brands narrow their focus and cut brand investment, the result is long, slow decline over years. Our clients were so focused on month-to-month sales fluctuations versus their big rival that they never noticed the long-term, decline.

The lesson? In marketing, remember that you're always waltzing with more than one partner.

HOW TO THINK ABOUT YOUR COMPETITION

2 minute checklist

o   Be vigilant. Ask: What are people doing
    instead of buying my brand? What *might* they do?

o   Track and pay attention to market share, not just sales.
    It's a much better performance metric.

o   Look at long-term trends. The movements that really matter
    often take place over years.

o   Don't define your competitive set too tightly. Real people
    don't see any difference between 'chocolate countlines' (like Snickers)
    and 'chocolate straightlines' (like M&M's).

o   Don't just use the definition that's been used for years. Markets are less
    segmented than you think. You compete with *every* brand in the market
    to some extent.

o   The threat from competitors is largely a matter of *size*. Your biggest
    competitors will be the biggest brands in the market. Even if you think
    they're in a different segment.

o   But watch out. Small brands en masse can have a bigger market share
    than brand leaders, and so be the main competition.

o   Watch out for threats from *beyond* your immediate category too.
    Your big threat may come from a 'disruptive' competitor that
    meets consumer needs in a new way.

o   Threats are also opportunities. If you're a small brand, don't box
    yourself in with 'niche thinking'. If you're a big brand, you can
    grow the category, or extend beyond it.

THE IMPORTANCE OF MARKET SHARE
FINANCIAL SERVICES BRAND

Useful case study

This financial services company measured short-term sales in exquisite detail, but had no system in place for tracking long-term market share trends. They didn't think it mattered, saying 'we're not selling baked beans here you know'. When they looked at this data, however, it showed the brand had been losing ground to competitors for years. And falling comms budgets were part of the problem…

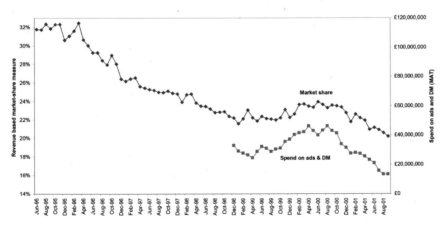

**Financial brand X:
market share vs comms spend**

HOW ~~NOT~~ TO THINK ABOUT LOYALTY

'If you want loyalty buy a dog'
Little Axe

We need to 'grow the brand by increasing loyalty'. Or 'change the brand image to improve brand loyalty'. We've all seen these objectives. Marketing is obsessed by loyalty. Does it matter though?

A London Business School survey showed that company boards regard loyalty as the single most important measure of brand health. Data from the IPA Databank suggests that campaigns with brand loyalty objectives outnumber those with a penetration objective by 2:1. Chasing loyalty seems embedded in marketing orthodoxy – its merit beyond question.

But we should question it. Because research backs us up. According to the IPA Databank again, most loyalty campaigns don't work. And on the rare occasions when they do work, they mostly do so by increasing penetration, not loyalty. There are hardly any examples of effective ad campaigns that worked primarily through improvements in loyalty. Unpick famous 'loyalty' cases, such as Tesco or O2, and the story usually turns out to be about penetration, not loyalty. And failure to improve brand loyalty is not just an advertising problem. It's been estimated that two thirds of all 'Customer Relationship Marketing' (CRM) programmes fail too.

This shouldn't surprise anyone familiar with marketing literature. Ehrenberg and disciples have reported similar findings for over 50 years. Across markets, they've found that brands all have remarkably similar (and low) levels of 'loyalty' as measured by things such as the share of category requirement. And, most importantly, loyalty in this sense is very resistant to change. When brands do grow, it's nearly all through penetration.

As Ehrenberg said: 'Most of your brand's users use other brands most of the time.' There's not much you can do to change this.

But the marketing community largely ignores Ehrenberg, preferring instead to listen to management consultancies like Bain, who've claimed to have 'proved' the importance of loyalty. Unfortunately, their research seems to have been based mainly on thought experiments, not empirical data. Bain showed that *if* companies could improve loyalty among existing customers, then they'd generate fantastic profits. But they didn't actually show that loyalty strategies *are* successful in the real world. It's a bit like saying that *if* you could turn lead into gold, then you'd get rich.

Why was the 'Fool's Gold' of loyalty so irresistible? Perhaps partly because Bain's research appeared at a time of recession (the early 1990s) when marketers were already in a mood of 'keep what you have'. And the myth then found support from direct marketing companies interested in new income streams from CRM and loyalty programmes. Maybe the explanation lies in the word itself: 'loyalty' just sounds like something you can't get enough of.

So, is loyalty irrelevant? Well that depends on what you mean. If you mean strengthening people's warmth towards the brand, then of course loyalty matters.

But conventional 'loyalty' metrics, such as frequency of purchase among existing users or customer retention rates, are poor ways to measure the strength of that brand relationship. And marketers who mistake them for measures of true brand loyalty tend to waste lots of money – on the wrong messages, in the wrong channels, to the wrong people.

To maximise growth and profitability, talking to your existing customers isn't enough. You need to talk to everyone in your category – customers and potential customers – and you need to do this with communication that strengthens people's relationship with your brand, and their willingness to pay for it. That's true loyalty. And that's where the gold lies.

HOW TO THINK ABOUT LOYALTY

2 minute checklist

o   'Brand loyalty' is a vague concept that can't
     really be measured. Use more precise language
     to describe the feelings and behaviours you want
     to provoke.

o   Use behavioural metrics such as frequency and weight of
     purchase, average spend per transaction, share of category
     requirement, retention rates, repurchase rates and cross-selling
     rates.

o   Don't be seduced by the 'loyalty myth'. The idea that brands can
     succeed with a small number of intensely loyal customers is appealing,
     but false.

o   Think of loyalty more as an open marriage. Very few people are
     exclusively loyal to one brand. And these true loyalists don't matter
     much in terms of sales and profit.

o   Don't think of penetration and loyalty as separate. They are really
     just two aspects of the same thing: propensity to buy.

o   Don't expect penetration and loyalty to move independently.
     When brands grow, penetration and loyalty always
     increase together.

o   But remember: penetration is always a lot
    more responsive to marketing than loyalty.

o   So don't make loyalty your primary focus. Loyalty
    rates don't vary much. And loyalty strategies aren't very
    effective.

o   Focus more on penetration. This is the main driver of growth.

o   More generally, aim to increase demand among 'customers'
    and 'non-customers' alike. Talk to everyone who buys the category.

o   This means you need to plan and budget for scale.

o   And have creative ideas that appeal to people who don't care
    about you.

o   Don't forget: supporting higher prices is usually more profitable
    than just increasing volume. So price sensitivity may be the best loyalty
    measure of all.

PROFITABLE LOYALTY MARKETING
O2

Useful case study

In 2004, O2 recognised that people were fed up with the aggressive acquisition-driven marketing typical of the mobile phone category. And so they decided to do things differently. Overtly, their new comms strategy was to focus on their existing customers, highlighting the improved service, loyalty rewards and other benefits that they were offering to them. The results were spectacular, with an ROI of 80:1.

However, this was not really a profitable loyalty marketing campaign as such. The campaign ran in mass media, and so most of the people who saw it were not O2 customers. Yes, loyalty metrics like churn and willingness to recommend improved, but the main effect was to recruit new customers. As the company concluded: 'Talking to existing customers proved to be a more effective acquisition strategy than the previous acquisition approach.'

Scratch the surface, and many other examples of successful 'loyalty' campaigns (eg Tesco, Sainsbury's) turn out to be penetration cases in disguise.

Notes:

_____

_____

_____

_____

_____

_____

_____

_____

HOW ~~NOT~~ TO 'CONVERT' PEOPLE

'Advertising is in an odd position: its strongest protagonists think it has
extraordinary powers and its severest critics believe them.
Both are wrong'
Andrew Ehrenberg

'Conversion' is everywhere these days.
Whether a brand campaign or a targeted
digital one, we're asked to 'convert'
people: from believing X to believing
Y; from rejectors to prospects; from
customers into loyalists. You'd think we
were missionaries. Not marketers.

This religious-conversion language is
dangerous. 'Conversion' implies a world
where people have clear beliefs, leading
to stable, defined behaviour patterns:
you're a customer or a non-customer;
promiscuous or a loyalist; a Pepsi buyer
or a Coke buyer.

Market research data seems to back this
up. Ask people whether they believe
Pepsi tastes better than Coke, and
most people will give a definite answer.

Track their responses over time, and
behaviour and beliefs seem to move
together. Armed with this view of the
world, evangelical marketing seems
natural. Spread the gospel of Pepsi's
taste, and some will hear the call and
switch from Coke.

Trouble is, the real world doesn't work
like this.

Our 'beliefs' about brands are nowhere
near as stable and consistent as we
think. As Ehrenberg-Bass's work with
re-contact surveys has shown, individual
opinions about brands are much more
volatile than top-line tracking data
suggests.

The overall percentage of people who

agree 'Pepsi tastes better than Coke' might stay the same from survey to survey. But that doesn't mean that *individual* respondents are answering the same way each time. Look at the data more closely, and you'll see that people answer research questions in a 'probabilistic' way. They may lean slightly in favour of one brand or another, but they don't have fixed beliefs.

Behaviour patterns are similarly fluid and messy. We like to think that people divide into distinct buying groups. But look at long runs of data, and you'll find that real-life buying behaviour is much more 'agnostic'. Buyers of premium brands also buy Own Label; low-fat buyers also buy full fat; Coke buyers buy Pepsi.

Our opinions about brands fluctuate depending on mood and occasion. And so do our brand choices. In the morning, we feel healthy and go for low fat. In the afternoon, we want chocolate.

And conscious beliefs have less influence on real people's behaviour than most marketers think. When brands grow, brand image scores do tend to improve. But the causality mainly goes the other way: purchases affect brand image more than brand image affects sales.

So don't talk 'conversion'. Most people don't have strong beliefs about brands. In fact, most don't think about brands at all. At least not consciously. That's why rational messages have so little influence on people.

And we rarely convert from one brand to another in a Damascene way. The best we can hope for is weak loyalty of habit; a slight tendency to choose a brand over rivals. Infrequent buys like cars or a new bank account might seem different. But the slow rate of switching here is just down to inertia. The kind of true commitment implied by 'conversion' is rare.

This is another of those situations where we need to step out of a 'tidy' marketing world into the messier world of real life. So forget the quasi-religious talk. Marketing isn't religion. A little agnosticism is a better mindset.

HOW TO THINK ABOUT CONVERSION

2 minute checklist

o   Think 'nudging', not 'conversion'. Our
    main job is to increase the probability of people
    choosing a brand within a repertoire.

o   Remember: real people don't think consciously about
    brands much. Their opinions about brands are surprisingly
    fluid and similar. And so they buy more than one brand in a
    category.

o   Don't think about your brand 'buyers' and 'non-buyers' as different
    people. Most people will have probably bought your brand before
    (unless it's new).

o   Don't talk about 'our brand buyers'. You don't own them. They buy
    other brands too.

o   Don't write briefs with objectives for advertising to 'make people
    do X' or 'get people to do Y'.

o   Watch your language. Avoid words like 'persuade', 'convert', 'recruit',
    'acquire', 'switch', 'swap' and 'exchange'.

o   Use words like 'remind', 'associate', 'feel' and
    'nudge' instead.

o   Remember: advertising influences people as a
    weak force, not a strong one.
o   This nudging process needs continual reinforcing. So plan
    comms to sustain it.
o   Don't overly focus on brand image scores. They don't move
    much. They don't show much difference between brands. And
    when they do move, it's usually just a reflection of brand size.
o   So beware of any KPIs which aim for big changes in brand image
    scores.
o   Target situations and states of mind, not segments. Make yours
    the brand that people are most likely to choose when they're
    doing X, feeling Y, or want to be Z.

HOW ~~NOT~~ TO DEAL WITH 'ALIENATION'

'Mostly, people either don't much like things or do quite like things. And the things they do quite like, they tend to buy quite regularly because they quite like them'
Jeremy Bullmore

One word crops up a lot on creative briefs: 'alienation'. Just recently, a brief for a new campaign cautioned: 'We want to appeal to new, younger soft cheese users, without "alienating" existing loyal users.'

Alienating 'loyal' customers obviously sounds bad news for any communication. But does it really happen? We've been evaluating advertising for years, and can't think of a single campaign that appealed to new users but actively turned regular users away. Nor has any campaign ever 'alienated' us enough to stop us buying the brand.

Fear of alienating existing customers is

understandable. But don't worry about it. Because it's based on two flawed ideas about how marketing works.

First, despite what you might think, real people don't have strong opinions about brands. They just don't care enough to feel alienated by them. Or have strong feelings about them – good or bad. Working in our world, that's hard to understand.

Secondly, brand users are not different from non-users. Empirical data shows that, within a given category, the 'non-users' you want to attract are pretty similar to the users you're worried about alienating. In fact, it's usually misleading to call them 'non-users'. In most cases, they've probably happily bought your brand before. It's just that they don't buy it often.

So, you can't come up with comms that appeal to non-users and 'alienate' users. Because they're basically the same people. And even if they're not, and you're going for a radical repositioning, habits are hard to break. People who're regular, long-term users of your brand are unlikely to defect just because they don't much like a new ad.

Many years ago, Super Noodles was radically repositioned away from children's tea-time food to post-pub blokes' snack. Some great irreverent ads were made, showing for example a dog licking the noodles off a plate. The client sensibly thought the risk of alienating regular-buying mums was low. And they were right. Children's tea use went up as much as night-time bloke snacks. Good ads tend to work for everyone.

A lot of this alienation paranoia is fuelled by the artificial nature of market research. Force people to analyse a new, provocative ad, and you'll see signs of 'alienation' in your research. People, by and large, don't like change. They prefer the ads they're used to.

Early in the 'Love/Hate' Marmite campaign, an ad showed a couple on a first date going back 'for coffee'. After eating toast and Marmite in the kitchen, the girl returns to the sofa. They kiss. Her boyfriend retches violently at the Marmite taste.

Most people in research thought it was hilarious. But older Marmite users didn't. You could say it 'alienated' them. But the ad ran. And the older users changed their view when they saw how popular it was. In fact, it turned out to be the 'lift-off' ad of the now-famous campaign, awarded for its creativity and for its results. Market research overestimates people's resistance to change and boldness, and underestimates 'herd effects'.

Alienation worry isn't just wrong, it's also dangerous. Because it can kill the bold, penetration-gaining ideas that you need for brand growth. So relax: it's actually quite hard to win friends and alienate people.

HOW TO THINK ABOUT ALIENATION

2 minute checklist

o Marketing that genuinely upsets people
   is probably a bad idea. Social media fans these
   flames. Think carefully about who you might offend.

o But look behind the headlines, and often the number of
   complaints is low. Sales may not suffer. Controversy can
   even be helpful (up to a point), by increasing salience.

o When it comes to ads, though, remember that real people don't
   much care about them. So negative effects are rare.

o We know of no evidence of any advertising that has had a negative
   effect on sales.

o Don't worry about 'alienation'. Negative effects among existing buyers
   but not new buyers or vice versa won't happen; we can't think of
   any examples.

o So don't hold back from bold, provocative ideas through fear of
   alienation. You should be much more fearful of indifference —
   and that's wonderfully liberating creatively.

o Remember: people are naturally resistant to
   change. Psychologists call this 'status quo bias'. This
   is different from 'alienation' but can be confused with it.
   Look out for this when researching new ideas.

o People are far more influenced by the opinions of others
   than we think. Remember: what looks like a controversial idea
   in research can be a massive hit in time, if enough people swing
   behind it.

o The easiest way to alienate people is aggressive marketing. Make
   your communications appealing or useful (or both). Don't pester
   people.

Notes:

_____

_____

_____

_____

_____

_____

_____

_____

PRODUCT, PRICE AND PLACE

'Too much of today's marketing is One P marketing'

Philip Kotler

TWO

INTRODUCTION

Marketing has traditionally been defined in terms of the four 'Ps': Product, Price, Place (meaning distribution) and Promotion (everything from in-store activity to advertising).

As planners, we can perhaps be forgiven for overly focusing on the 'Promotion' bit of marketing. But it's interesting how many marketing people now also seem to view their role mainly as 'promotion'.

Communication is obviously important for brand success. But econometrics show that the effects of the other three Ps are usually even more important for sales and profit. Without the right products, at the right price, in the right places, advertising is powerless. As planners we need to understand this.

So, before we focus on communication in Chapter 3, here we step back and consider the three other important sales levers from a planner's perspective. What's the role of new products; should we focus on them or the 'old' products? Why does distribution matter, and how might communication affect it? Is price promotion a good thing, or something to avoid?

These are questions planners need to think about; long before thinking about ads.

BRANDS CANNOT LIVE FOREVER

'Buildings age and become dilapidated. Machines wear out. People die. But what lives on are the brands'
Hector Laing, ex-Chairman, Nabisco

Some years ago, just before the 'Global Financial Crisis', we were talking to institutional investors about the effects of advertising spend on profit. At the end of our presentation, one of them asked a question. Yes, he understood the need for marketing support when launching a brand. But surely this was less important in the later stages of the brand life cycle?

But brands don't have 'life cycles'. This myth is a dangerous one, damaging the interests of brand owners and investors. Products certainly have life cycles; we're not using the iPhone 3G anymore. And product categories can have life cycles, too. Typewriters, fax machines, cassette players… all made obsolete by the march of technology.

But brands are different from products. A brand is a collective mental construct: a network of shared feelings and associations. Those associations can change over time and attach themselves to an array of different products. So there's no inherent reason why a brand should have a fixed shelf life at all. In fact, many of today's top grocery brands (Heinz, Kellogg's, Hovis) are centenarians.

Two things, though, are key to brand longevity. The brand must receive sustained marketing support. Andrex, for example, has benefited from years of nurturing through its puppy advertising. And then the brand must evolve and grow to reflect changing market conditions. As an extreme example, mobile phone company Nokia started life in 1865 as a Finnish wood pulp company.

Well-managed brands can often last longer than the companies that own them: Dulux has outlived ICI. Of course, as with biological evolution, extinctions do occur. Market conditions can change suddenly, leaving all brands in a category in a vulnerable position. But poor management is more often the culprit. If there is any 'life cycle', it's a brand management cycle.

In the first exciting phase of this cycle, the brand is launched with strong marketing support. All graphs trend upwards. The effects of marketing are easy to see. And budgets are easy to justify.

But, however well managed, eventually sales will plateau for a while. This is phase 2. Marketing is still working. But now its job is to maintain the brand's hard-earned market share and defend it against competitive threats. Unfortunately, this maintenance job is nowhere near as sexy as phase 1. So it tends to get less management attention. Plus, the effects of marketing are harder to see. So sooner or later, budgets come under attack.

And that leads to phase 3. Now, cuts in the marketing budget cause sales to decline. Brand owners then panic and try to restore volumes with price promotions. These deliver short-term sales, but they damage brand image and worsen the long-term sales decline. This makes marketing expenditure even harder to justify, leading to a vicious circle of budget cuts and plummeting sales. The result? The brand often just withers away.

The term 'brand life cycle' makes all this seem inevitable. In fact, this fatal cycle of poor management even gained a kind of respectability through the enthusiastic adoption by marketers of the famous 'Boston Matrix' (whereby analysis identified 'Cash Cows' generating funds to put behind 'Stars').

But this matrix was meant to be applied to categories — not brands. Labelling a brand a 'Cash Cow' was the first step to an inevitable lingering death.

Recessions are a particularly dangerous time for brands: they're one of those periods when 'mass extinctions' tend to occur. But by debunking the myth of the brand life cycle, we can at least avoid making things worse. Remember: death is optional for brands. If not, unfortunately, for the rest of us.

HOW TO THINK ABOUT LIFE CYCLES

2 minute checklist

o   Aim for brand immortality.

o   Remember: advertising is forever, not just for
     the launch.

o   Prepare the finance director and other sceptical board
     members for the day when sales begin to stall. Show them
     why they'll need to keep investing in the brand.

o   Planning guru Paul Feldwick has a useful analogy to help here.
     Think of advertising as like the engines of a plane: they're not just
     important to get you up, they're needed to *keep* you up too.

o   Commit money for this long-term maintenance task.

o   Simple 'Share of Voice' (SOV)/'Share of Market' (SOM) calculations
     can help estimate how much you need to spend just to stand still.

o   Econometrics and regional tests can also help by showing what
     might happen without advertising.

o   Beware setting budgets as a fixed percentage of sales. If sales go
     down, that means you'll automatically cut your budgets, leading
     to a death spiral.

o   Understand that when budgets are cut,
    sales *will* go down. Maybe your sales can 'glide' for
    a year, but two years without engines can
    kill a brand.
o   Competitors can use this death spiral time to move in
    and kill your brand. Conversely, if your competitors cut their
    budgets, seize the opportunity to deal them a killer blow.
o   Be clear about any Boston Matrix analyses. Do you face a
    declining *category*? If so, try changing how the category is used,
    or shifting your brand to a different category.
o   Or do you just face declining *share* in a healthy category? If so,
    that's your fault. Do something about it.

HOW ~~NOT~~ TO MANAGE YOUR PRODUCT PORTFOLIO

'Coca-Cola scraps its "healthy" low-sugar Coke Life in UK after sales of the green cans and bottles nosedive'
MailOnline, April 2017

Tried to buy mouthwash recently?

We have. And it's not easy. The brand leader alone comes in 15 different variants, all available in different sizes. Faced with this baffling array of choices, you either randomly pick one, or just give up.

Why do brand owners do this? Why swamp us with so many options? The standard argument is that product innovation and 'consumer choice' are inherently good things. I myself might not want a tooth-whitening mouthwash, but someone, somewhere, might. By constantly tweaking and expanding their product range, brands are therefore helping us to 'satisfy our

needs'. But often the real reason for all this innovation is a bit less worthy. Usually, brands just want something new to say.

Once again, the problem here is the 'message myth'. Most marketers wrongly believe their job is to 'persuade' people with compelling product messages. And if you follow this rational persuasion model, then nothing works like 'new news'. People quickly run out of things to say about their old products, so 'message' marketers tend to focus on new ones. And a steady pipeline of new products gives something new to talk about every year. Retailers love offering customers something new, and developing new products can help brands gain more shelf space too. And people do like trying new things. Thus each new product launch gives sales a little short-term boost.

This approach can work well if the product is really ground-breaking. But most new products aren't. At least, not in mature markets like mouthwash. So, the trade will give the latest variant shelf space for a while. Yes, some of us will try it once. But usually, that's about it. As a result, most new products fail. And marketers find themselves on a treadmill of pointless pseudo-innovation. Worse, they neglect the core products that generate most of their profits, because there's nothing new to say about them.

We came across a textbook example of this recently. The brand in question was category leader, offered a huge range of products, and was constantly launching new ones. Each year, a new campaign supported the latest variant. And each year, overall market share slipped further downwards. The brand's owners were baffled: they'd followed all the rules of message marketing, but sales kept falling. Meanwhile, a rival brand took a different tack. They concentrated on the core, established products that generated most sales in this category.

And because there was nothing new to say about those products, they didn't bother to try. Instead they focused on how people felt about them. By building up a strong emotional connection with customers, their brand achieved strong growth every year, without expensive 'New Product Development' (NPD) or price promotions.

The Foster's IPA paper, which won the 2014 Grand Prix, tells a similar story. Foster's was in trouble, losing market share in a declining sector. There were some new products in the pipeline, but brand owners Heineken chose instead to focus on the core product. And rather than trying to find something new to say about the beer, they concentrated on how young blokes felt about the brand. The solution was remarkably old-fashioned – a series of funny TV ads featuring a couple of likeable Australian lads – but the sales results were stunning.

Our new news message from all this? Support the core and ignore the new.

HOW TO THINK ABOUT NEW PRODUCTS

2 minute checklist

o   Focus on genuinely ground-breaking
     innovation. If you get it right, you may not need
     to advertise it much, as Amazon, Google and Uber all
     found in their early days.

o   And don't forget the power of 'Old Product Development'.
     Putting ketchup into squeezy bottles breathed new life into a
     100-year-old product.

o   But don't waste money advertising 'trivial' NPD. Save spend for the
     game-changers.

o   Watch out for the warning signs in research. People tend to be
     politely positive about new variants, even useless ones. If people
     say, 'It would be good for camping', kill it now.

o   Never launch a new product just because you want some
     'new news'. Make sure it satisfies some genuine functional or emotional
     need.

o   Focus NPD support on 'activation', close to the point of purchase.
     Think 10-second ads, posters outside supermarkets, and
     point-of-sale activity. Sales teams and retailers love this stuff.

o   Remember: advertising becomes *more*
    essential as brands mature, not less. That's why
    the big tech brands are all ramping their adspend now.

o   Always support your core products, regardless of NPD. It's
    where your volume is. And where most growth will probably
    come from too.

o   Don't underestimate the potential of your core products. They may
    seem less responsive to ads, but paybacks are usually higher, because
    volumes are bigger.

o   Think of the core as your brand gateway. Ads selling the core tend
    also to sell new products. The reverse isn't always true.

o   Don't worry about 'new news'. Ads for 'boring old products' like
    vanilla ice cream or white paint can still be highly effective, if
    they focus on the needs and feelings at the heart of the
    category.

GROWTH WITHOUT INNOVATION
MARMITE

Useful case study

To see how a venerable brand can keep on growing without significant NPD, take a look at the history of Marmite. This strange, salty black substance is a bit of a British institution: we've been spreading it on our toast at breakfast since 1902.

By the mid-1970s, Marmite looked like the epitome of a 'Cash Cow': highly profitable, but going nowhere in a category (spreads) that was shrinking. However, rather than sit back and rake in the cash, the brand's owners chose to invest. They more than doubled the advertising budget, and over the following years they doubled it again.

The result was a 25-year run of almost continual growth, despite continued category decline. There were precious few changes to product and packaging during that period, and the few tweaks that were made had little effect on sales, as the chart opposite shows. Rather, growth came from the core, driven by great advertising, culminating (from 1995 onwards) in the famous 'Love/Hate' campaign.

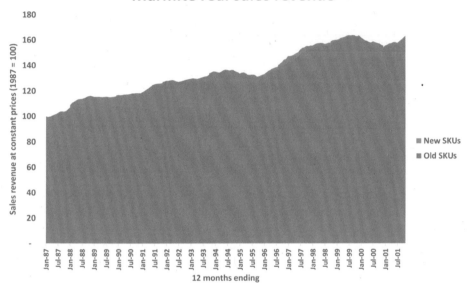

Marmite real sales revenue

Later on (in 2006), there was one significant product launch: a new squeezy plastic bottle. This was a real boon for Marmite lovers, because it made the notoriously viscous black goo easier and less messy to use and spread. Advertising this – the first genuine improvement in over 100 years – took sales of the core product to even higher levels; a classic example of Old Product Development.

HOW ~~NOT~~ TO THINK ABOUT DISTRIBUTION

'The consumer is loyal to the brand they can find'
John F Mars

A brand manager was once asked by *Marketing* magazine how they defined marketing. Their reply? 'It's about creating, communicating and delivering an engaging, consistent and clear message to a target audience.' Really? Since when did marketing just equal communication?

Marketing has traditionally been defined in terms of the four 'Ps': Product, Price, Place and Promotion. But it's interesting how many marketers these days seem to see their role as 'Promotion'. Or even more narrowly as 'communication'. Communication is obviously important. But econometrics show the effect of the other three Ps are often more important. Here we focus on perhaps the least talked about P: 'Place', meaning physical availability and distribution.

Distribution is important in an obvious sense: people need to be able to buy you. But it's not enough to just be 'available'. Behavioural economics shows that people are lazy, and all effort counts; thus the more widely and easily available you are, the more you'll sell. That's why Coke's aim is to be 'within an arm's reach of desire'.

Physical availability is in turn closely linked with what Byron Sharp calls 'mental availability' or salience: the ease with which a product comes to mind. Many people find out about a brand by seeing it in-store, not on TV. So simply seeing the product on display is one of the simplest and most effective forms of 'advertising'. Which is why pack design matters so much. Shelf wobblers, gondola ends and all the other paraphernalia of merchandising help. But sheer on-shelf ubiquity is probably the best way to ensure your brand is the first to spring to mind.

As well as boosting salience, distribution can create useful brand associations. By getting their brand into John Lewis's cafés, the makers of Plum baby food not only brought their product to the attention of upmarket mums, they also sent out a clear quality signal. Similarly, clever thinking about distribution can communicate things about value (selling your luxury car at a boat show makes it look more affordable) or usage (displaying your sauce next to barbecue food tells people how to use it).

Put all this together, and distribution has a big influence on sales. Econometrics show distribution tends to be the single biggest factor driving long-term growth for many brands. Yet lots of marketing people see distribution as outside their remit. In many cases, it's the responsibility of a different department.

That's a big lost opportunity. Thinking creatively about distribution can yield spectacular results, as companies such as Direct Line, Ocado and Apple have shown. And because few brands have anything like universal distribution, there's

nearly always scope for further growth this way. By harnessing new technology, like the Kindle or the iPhone. Or by thinking about old distribution methods in new ways, like selling headphones in vending machines. Or by delivering parcels via corner shops.

Of course, distribution and comms are closely linked, as various IPA Effectiveness papers have shown. Felix cat food is a good example. Over more than 25 years, advertising helped Felix gain distribution, both directly (by influencing retailers) and indirectly (by boosting rate of sale). This in turn helped the brand quintuple market share, boosting ROI from advertising by 50%.

Digital marketing allows marketers to advertise products and sell them directly, bringing Promotion and Place even closer together. And with mobile marketing, the dream of being 'within an arm's reach' is fast becoming a reality.

More than ever, marketers need to exploit the power of distribution. Few brands are so widely available that they can't significantly increase sales through thinking creatively about it. As John F Mars used to tell his colleagues: 'The consumer is loyal to the brand they can find.'

HOW TO THINK ABOUT DISTRIBUTION

2 minute checklist

o   Make your brand ubiquitous. Maximise
    distribution in existing outlets and think creatively
    about new ones: planes, offices, vending machines,
    street sellers etc.

o   Think about *how* and *when* people might access your brand,
    as well as where. Amazon is constantly looking for new ways to
    speed up deliveries, such as using lockers and smart key systems.

o   Don't underestimate the importance of just making things easy for
    buyers. Few people in the real world have the time or inclination to
    seek out your brand.

o   So make your brand *easy to find*. Think about siting in-store, size of
    display, whether yours is the first brand people see when they search
    online etc.

o   Understand your branded cues: design, logo, colour, pack shape
    etc. Don't muck around with these and confuse people.

o   Make your brand *easy to buy*. One-click ordering, pre-filled
    forms, automatic re-ordering – the principles of behavioural
    economics are important and useful here. London
    restaurant Bob Bob Ricard has a button at every

table marked 'Press for Champagne'!

o Make your brand *easy to choose*. Remove unnecessary options. Keep the choice architecture simple. Help people to know what they want before they go to choose.

o Consider the 'framing' implications of where your product is sold or not sold. What does it 'say' about your brand?

o Use advertising to help gain better distribution. It gives the sales force a story to tell, and retailers will be more favourable to them when they see how it boosts rate of sale.

o Use advertising to maintain distribution as well. Cutting ad budgets will depress rate of sale, turning retailers against you. If they de-list your product, it can be the end.

USING ADVERTISING TO SUPPORT DISTRIBUTION AND PRICE
FELIX CAT FOOD

Useful case study

Distribution and price generally have much bigger effects on sales than advertising. Making sure you sell the right product, at the right price, in all the right places is crucial. But advertising can help with all that, and the Felix case (outlined in a series of IPA papers) shows how.

Back in the late 1980s, Felix cat food was struggling to survive. One of the smallest brands in the category, with only 5% market share, Felix was on the point of being de-listed by the major supermarkets, who were keen to replace it with their Own Label products.

In a last-ditch attempt to save the brand, its owners relaunched it with new packaging and its first major ad campaign. The ads, featuring the adventures of Felix, a black and white cartoon cat, were a hit with cat owners, and sales rose dramatically. Felix became one of the fastest growing FMCG (Fast-Moving Consumer Goods) brands in Britain, and eventually overtook market leader Whiskas. Market share increased by a factor of five.

The rise of Felix

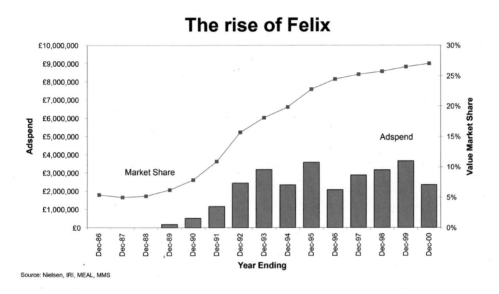

Source: Nielsen, IRI, MEAL, MMS

The huge increase in demand that the Felix ads created had two interesting effects on the business. First, the ads reduced price sensitivity, allowing the brand's owners to gradually increase price from the bottom end of the market to the top. Secondly, the ads made the brand much more profitable for retailers, who therefore allocated it more shelf space, boosting sales still further. A textbook example of how advertising can make other marketing jobs much easier.

HOW ~~NOT~~ TO CHANGE PRICE

'Price is what you pay. Value is what you get'
Warren Buffett

The promotions and incentives market have had a bumper recession, fuelled by discounts, two-for-one deals and websites such as VoucherCodes and Groupon. Will we ever need to pay for both pizzas in a restaurant again?

The 'less than full price' trend predates recent economic problems, and has accounted for an unrelenting increase in share of marketing budgets for years. In many sectors, trade spend dwarfs other communication spend. Of course, there's a seductive charm in price offers. But dangers lurk beneath the allure of short-term sales increases. People tend not to stop to analyse or think much about these.

Let's start with the short-term, good news. Analysis of Electronic Point of Sale (EPOS) data often suggests that price-related promotions increase short-term sales by 30–70%. But many of these apparently 'incremental' sales are not. Some may be cannibalised from other pack sizes of the same brand. Others may be diverted from stores where the brand is not on promotion. And others could be just future sales brought forward by the offer. In fact, an analysis by IRI suggests that 84% of promotions are unprofitable, even in the short term.

Things get even worse when we look beyond immediate effects. Because promotions tend to encourage people to stockpile (buying one pack for now and one for the freezer is typical supermarket promotional behaviour), sales often slump after promotions end. When this is taken into account, net short-term sales effects are often close to zero.

But surely, brands do all this to encourage

new users to give them a try. Or to keep existing users buying? Well, research has failed to find much evidence of any long-term benefit from price promotions. They do little to encourage either trial (most people who buy on promotion have already tried the brand) or 'loyalty' (buyers tend to be less brand loyal: they buy by the voucher, not the brand). In fact, promotions are pretty inefficient. Only 5% of potential buyers are likely to be exposed to any promotional offer in any one week. The evidence is that promotions can be damaging in the long run, tarnishing a brand's image, increasing price sensitivity and reducing brand loyalty. This explains why brands that rely heavily on promotions tend to be less profitable, particularly big brands in mature markets.

And it gets worse. Despite the negative effect on profits, promotions tend to escalate. When the 'high' of one promotion ends and sales slump, it's tempting to go for one more promotional 'fix'. But promotions are easily copied, so competitors follow suit, leading to promotional 'wars'. As promotional activity escalates, people become less responsive to it, and deals must become ever more generous to be effective. Left unchecked, this runaway promotional warfare can commoditise the whole category. People stop buying by brand, instead buying solely on the basis of price and offers. The only beneficiaries are retailers and Own Label products.

Of course, not all promotions are a bad thing. They can be useful in some contexts, like encouraging trial for new products or categories. There's also evidence they work well for indulgent impulse buys, like chocolate or crisps, where they help increase consumption (whether that's a socially useful thing is another matter).

Different promotional mechanics also have different benefits. Price promotions are only suitable for price-sensitive items where variable costs are low. Well thought-out promotions may have better effects, especially if used in a way that helps build brand equity (eg a PG Tips 'Show Me the Monkey' cash prize promotion, where people also win knitted monkeys and monkey mugs). But, for most brand owners, BOGOFs (Buy One Get One Frees) and discounts are just a great way of handing profits straight back to the customer.

So enjoy those free pizzas. They may not be around for long.

HOW TO THINK ABOUT PRICE

2 minute checklist

o   Beware the lure of price promotions.
They're usually unprofitable and damage
brands. Ask yourself some questions before you
promote.

o   Can you really increase category consumption? Promos
can make people eat more chocolate, but won't make them
use more loo roll.

o   Have people tried your product already? If it's been around for
a while, you won't get much trial.

o   How big is your market share? If you're a big brand, you'll just
cannibalise existing sales.

o   How big are your variable costs? Promos only make money when
costs are low. Remember: promos can increase revenue but
still lose money, because of reduced profit.

o   Is your product easy to store? If people stock up when you
promote, sales will slump afterwards.

o   Are you a retailer? Promote a few selected products only,
to draw in shoppers. Get the manufacturers to fund your
promos, if you can.

o   Are you a manufacturer? Negotiate hard with retailers

who insist on promotions. Try to get something
in return, like increased facings, better siting, in-store
display etc.

o   Are promotional sales incremental, or just brought forward?
    Use econometrics to find out.

o   What will price promotions say about your brand? Repeated
    promos just teach people to buy cheap, and are particularly
    damaging for premium brands.

o   Consider non-price promotions, such as competitions or free gifts.
    These are often more profitable.

o   Is your base price right? Stable sales at low everyday prices may
    be better than promo spikes.

o   If you are going to promote, use the right mechanic. If the aim is
    to gain trial, use trial sizes. If the aim is to get regular customers,
    use 'Money Off Next Purchase'.

o   Don't be too generous. A modest discount may be almost as
    effective as a deep one. Really generous promotions
    can be ruinous.

THE DANGER OF DISCOUNTING
MULTINATIONAL RETAILER

Useful case study

Although price promotions tend to be destructive for manufacturers, they can be useful for retailers. Enticing offers on much loved brands can act as 'loss leaders' which, while not profitable in themselves, increase store traffic, and hence overall sales. And if the retailer can bully the manufacturer into funding all this, so much the better.

But sometimes retailers take it too far, and end up damaging their own business. The chart opposite shows sales growth for the key European markets of a multinational retailer from 2008 to 2010. Different countries pursued different strategies during this period. Some increased advertising Share of Voice (SOV), some cut it; some did lots of discounting, others not so much.

Sales growth vs marketing strategy

	Markets where share of voice was cut	Markets where share of voice was increased
Markets where discounts were modest and/or falling	+13% growth	+15% growth
Markets where discounts were heavy and/or rising	+2% growth	+9% growth

Figures show increase in sales per store, key European markets, 2008 – 2010

As you can see, advertising clearly stimulated sales growth (Column 2 vs Column 1), but discounting actually *reduced* it (Row 2 vs Row 1). Excessive promotion was making shoppers more price sensitive, and reluctant to buy anything there that wasn't on deal.

Notes:

_____

_____

_____

_____

_____

_____

_____

BRAND AND
COMMUNICATION

'I will *not* have my company's fine products endorsed by a rodent'

Quaker Oats client

THREE •————————————————

INTRODUCTION

We've looked at Product, Price and Place. Now we move on to the fourth 'P': Promotion (or what we now usually call 'Marketing Communications').

This chapter is a mix of articles. All look at the real-world context for communication, not the distorted view of reality it's easy to succumb to at the planning coalface.

It's really hard to keep this perspective. But vital that we do. Picasso said it took him a lifetime to paint like a child. Many of us perhaps never spend long enough in our jobs to think like a real person.

In this chapter, we remind ourselves of some easy-to-forget communication fundamentals: real people don't care about brands; they don't spend time thinking about brands; they don't have high interest in brands; and they

certainly don't want 'relationships' with brands. In fact, the main reason people choose any particular brand is so they *don't* have to waste time thinking about them.

This stuff all has profound implications for how we plan and think about communication. Creatively, this reality is wonderfully liberating. It means we don't need 'messages'. We don't need to 'make sense'. We don't need to bother trying to build deep relationships with buyers. And we can forget about trying to find anything 'differentiated' from competitors to talk about.

Get it right, and this stuff can unlock growth, increase margins and help clients make money. But get it wrong, and you'll end up wasting their money on ineffective communication.

HOW ~~NOT~~ TO THINK ABOUT BRAND CHOICE

'Humans are to independent thinking as cats are to swimming – we can do it when we have to, but we'd much prefer not to'
Daniel Kahneman

At a conference some months ago, we were approached by a marketer responsible for a big global brand. She had a dilemma: 'What's the "functional hierarchy" consumers use to choose a soft drink? Do they start by deciding what size can they want, then decide on flavour, then choose a brand? Or do they do it in a different order?'

When marketers talk like this, alarm bells ring. A moment's reflection, and it's obvious no-one in the real world makes decisions in this rational, sequential way.

Try it. Go to the supermarket. Stand in front of the soft drinks. Now try to choose between them in the way the

marketer questioned. Weigh up the different factors. Then work your way through them, one by one. How long did that take? Now, imagine doing that for every item on your shopping list. How long would your weekly trip to Sainsbury's take? Decision-making flowcharts and functional hierarchies look nice and tidy on a PowerPoint chart. But real-life decisions just aren't made like this.

Anyone with any understanding of real people knows the way we make decisions is illogical, contradictory and messy. We're guided by feelings, intuitions, hunches and habits. We say one thing. Then do another. We're more Homer Simpson than Mr Spock.

Academia now is giving us hard evidence for all this. Psychologists and economists paint a different picture of how people really make choices.

Most mental processing that guides our actions is associative not logical. Emotional not rational. Conscious, verbal thinking plays a minor role most of the time. And the parallel processing architecture of the brain makes a mockery of sequential flowcharts like the one the marketer described.

People just don't spend time thinking about products and services they buy. Most decision making is gut feel. Even for big-ticket items like cars and houses. Our choices are steered by intuitions and feelings that none of us really understand. And conscious thinking is mostly a matter of cross-checking or rubber stamping intuitive choices.

We may not like this, because we spend so much of our day wrapped up in the intricacies of our brands. But real people don't think much about brands, categories or markets. In fact, humans don't do much thinking about *any* of their actions.

So why does all this matter? Well, a client recently told us that he spent most of his marketing budget on in-store promotional activity. Because that's where most decisions are made. When we asked him how he knew that, he replied that research showed most people didn't know which brand they were going to buy before they entered the store. They hadn't come to a conscious, rational decision outside the shop. So logically, they *must* be doing it inside. Once you understand how people really make choices, it's obvious this kind of thinking is flawed and leads to bad marketing.

It seems to us that this 'thinking myth' is one of the most dangerous and pervasive in marketing nowadays. It explains our continued misguided obsession with 'messages', 'propositions' and 'Reasons to Believe' (RTBs). It's the reason why so much research is useless. And it leads to advertising that expensively underperforms.

The implications are huge.

HOW TO THINK ABOUT BRAND CHOICE
SYSTEM 1 AND SYSTEM 2

Useful summary

Our brains have two different ways of processing data and making decisions. Both play their part in determining the products we buy, and the brands we choose. Here's our quick guide to what Daniel Kahneman calls 'Thinking Fast' ('System 1') and 'Thinking Slow' ('System 2').

SYSTEM 1	SYSTEM 2
Dominant mode of thought > 95% of brain activity	**Secondary mode of thought** < 5% of brain activity
Fast and powerful Honed by millions of years of evolution	**Slow and limited** A more recent addition
Parallel processing Processes millions of inputs simultaneously	**Serial processing** Processes selected items in sequence
Effortless Always on	**Effortful** Hard to sustain
Scans *all* sensory inputs But can be primed by System 2 to watch out for things of interest	**Selective attention** Guided by System 1 feelings, associations & intuitions
Unconscious & automatic responses Associative & heuristic processing. Experienced as feelings, intuitions & habits	**Conscious & deliberate thought** Can follow learned rules of thought, eg maths, logic & legal reasoning
Primary decision-making mechanism Strong influence on System 2. Can be influenced by System 2	**Secondary cross-checking mechanism** Mostly post-rationalises System 1 decisions. Can sometimes overrule System 1

SYSTEM 1	SYSTEM 2
Vast memory capacity Durable memories. Long-term influence on behaviour	**Limited memory capacity** Quickly overwritten. Short-term influence on behaviour
Buying implications	
Does most of brand choice work. Not logical or rational. Some brands just *feel* more attractive	Only kicks in close to point of purchase. More likely to *prevent* buying than stimulate it
Makes purchase decision seamless & automatic. Choosing your brand should be a no-brainer	Be wary about trying to make people think; they don't like it, & won't thank you for it
Comms implications	
Trained, not taught. Brand building is about creating associations, feelings & habits through repeated exposure	Influenced by messages, arguments & information, but only late in decision-making process
Research implications	
Hard to research. System 1 dominates, but we're mostly unaware of its influence	Research exaggerates importance. We mistakenly attribute actions to System 2 – because it's what we're conscious of

HOW ~~NOT~~ TO BE INTERESTING

'There are no dull products, only dull writers'
David Ogilvy

We had a briefing for a new campaign the other day. It was for a financial product, and it started with an explanation of how the product worked. The briefing ended apologetically: 'This is, of course, a very low interest category'.

It's a familiar phrase to any of us who've worked on finance brands or utilities – classic 'low interest' categories. And it's often assumed too that these are 'rational' purchases. Implying other categories are more emotional and 'high interest'. But actually, we've always found it's best to think of *all* categories and brands as low interest. We spend our days immersed in the finer details of clients' products. But real people just don't care about any of this stuff.

As far as 'real people' are concerned, nearly *all* purchases are low interest.

People are interested in their families, friends, jobs, weekend plans and celebrity gossip – not brands or products. Occasionally, they may rouse themselves to consider which wine to buy for a special dinner. Or which mobile phone to buy for a teenage daughter's birthday. And everybody has a few purchases they're unusually picky about – a passion for shoes maybe. But most of us don't devote much brainpower to buying anything. We've got too many other more important or interesting things to think about.

And because we can't devote much mental effort to shopping, we rely on feelings, hunches and intuitions to guide our purchases. Even in so-called 'rational' categories. Psychologists tell us that most buying decisions are either too complex or too trivial to be made analytically. So people have to rely on emotions instead.

So, should we think of *all* categories as 'low interest' and 'emotional' then? Well, not quite. It's more helpful to think in terms of different moments and states of mind. During the buying process, people oscillate between long periods of low interest, when they're guided by feelings. Then short bursts of more intense interest, when rational thinking *can* play a role. The balance between (and timing of) these states is different for different people.

As communications experts, we need to be able to talk to people in both states. Create brands that stand out, even when people aren't interested in them. Create an emotional 'halo' to influence people who don't care about our products. And then provide rational arguments to convince the few people who do care. At the right time – and when they are interested.

If we do our jobs well, we can make anything interesting. The dynamic steering systems of big trucks seem as dull as it gets. Until along comes Jean-Claude Van Damme doing the splits between two huge moving Volvo trucks as the sun rises – and suddenly we're all interested in the amazing stability and precision of Volvo. And if we were ever in the market to buy a big truck in the future, Volvo would be the first brand to come to mind.

Adding interest to things that people don't care about is one of the most important functions of advertising. When you look at the Super Bowl ads, you'll see the way to do it is tap into things that people *do* care about: celebrities, animals, children, funny stories, music etc. These work just as well for finance or trucks as for beer or chocolate.

So next time someone calls a product 'low interest', remember that this is what makes our job so interesting.

HIGH AND LOW INTEREST MARKETING

2 minute checklist

o   Never dismiss a product or category as low
     interest.

o   Every brief is an opportunity for great work.
     Price comparison sites are pretty dull. Meerkats aren't.

o   Think in terms of high and low interest *mood states*. Not
     high and low interest categories.

o   Understand when people are interested in your brand or
     category, and when they're more interested in other things.

o   Remember: *all* categories and brands are low interest to most
     people most of the time.

o   Don't let that deter you. Talk to people long before they start
     thinking about buying. Brand building is a slow process.

o   Use creativity to influence people who're *not* interested in your brand,
     or what you have to say.

o   Don't *force* people to pay attention. Charming, memorable ads
     work better than 'hard sell'.

o   Be interested in what people *do* find
    interesting. What are they doing? Watching?
    Reading? Listening to? Searching for? Use this
    stuff to make the mundane interesting.

o   Talk to people in high attention states in a different
    way. At high interest times (eg about to
    buy a car) give them information efficiently.

o   Choose the right media for the right attention state. TV
    viewing is relaxed and low attention. Online is more 'lean
    forward'. Video is great for brand building. Text for detailed
    information.

NONSENSE DOES ~~NOT~~ WORK

'Don't make sense'
Paul Smith

Many years ago, we worked on the tea brand PG Tips. It had huge sales, and had led the UK market for decades. It had a famous, long-running campaign featuring tea-loving chimps. And the brand was bolstered by stable numbers of buyers, whose habits seemed ingrained. It was hard to see this situation changing much. They rarely do.

So when word got out that the main tea competitor, Tetley, had a bizarre new product up its sleeve, we and our client weren't unduly worried. PG Tips came in square tea bags, like the rest of the market in those days. Tetley's new tea idea was round bags. This made no sense at all to us. The tea would taste just the same, wouldn't it? We gave it a few months, at best. But how wrong we were. People loved the new round bags. And Tetley shot to brand leader in a year.

We were reminded of this story when we visited an exhibition celebrating the career of fashion designer and retailer Paul Smith. Among his mantras for successful design was: 'Don't make sense'.

He was right for marketing and advertising too. Tetley's tea bags made no logical 'sense' at all. But this didn't matter. People somehow liked the 'feeling' of their new round bags. They seemed friendlier, cosier, more tea-like. They even fitted more snugly into the bottom of your mug.

It seems to us that this story illustrates one of the great lessons in marketing: things don't always need to make sense. Often the biggest differences come from small things with no logic or function.

In one famous psychological experiment, people were asked to select a loaf of bread. The loaves were all identical. Except one had a random alphabet letter stamped on it. It made no 'sense' to choose that loaf over the others. But that's what people did. As Byron Sharp reminds us, it's often more important for brands to be distinctive than truly different functionally.

These minor differences seem to work best when they give us a little emotional 'reward'. We did some econometrics once on a cat food brand's digital marketing effectiveness. The most successful activity wasn't the price promotions. Or product information. It was a funny little animated cat app that people could play with on their mobiles when bored. This didn't 'make sense' at all. But it had the highest ROI of all activity.

Similarly, it didn't 'make sense' for Coke to sell bottles with people's names on them. It didn't make much sense for Cadbury to sell chocolate with a drumming gorilla. But when you do things that make people smile, they tend to buy your product.

There's a generosity of spirit about this stuff. The brand is giving us an 'emotional freebie'. And behavioural economics shows we get disproportionately excited about freebies. Especially stuff that we get here and now.

This helps explain the success of 'instant win' promotions. And why Waitrose had such success with their scheme offering free coffees to myWaitrose card customers. People much prefer a free latte *now* to collecting points for reductions on future buys. At one stage, Waitrose was apparently serving more coffees in the UK than anyone apart from McDonald's.

These little differences are just the kinds of things that get trimmed by rational, cost–benefit marketing. Because it's hard to say quite 'why' they work. Why names on bottles? Why a funny cat app? Why free coffees? But there's hard economic evidence that they do work very well. So next time you're presented with an idea that feels good but doesn't make sense, don't ask 'Why?' ask 'Why not?'

Remember: often in marketing, it's sensible not to make sense.

'IRRATIONAL' BUYING

2 minute checklist

o   Remember: we don't choose brands in logical, functional ways. Choices are often 'irrational', because decisions are led by System 1.

o   Never assume that having great products and prices is enough. Cognitive biases lead people to choose an 'inferior' brand, because they like the colour (say).

o   Understand these biases. Use them to your brand's advantage.

o   Harness the power of the 'mere exposure effect'. Remind people about your brand and sales will rise. Even if you've nothing to say.

o   Build 'mental availability'. Make sure your brand comes to mind quickly and easily.

o.   Use 'emotional priming'. People are more likely to buy brands that make them feel good.

o   Use the 'halo effect' to create these associations. If people like your ad, they'll like your brand.

o   Remember the fundamental rule of behavioural economics: little things mean a lot.

- o So don't dismiss the small or quirky –
  for NPD or communications. A little 'meaningless
  distinctive' can give brands real competitive edge.
- o Fight for the tiny executional details that have a big
  influence on effectiveness.
- o Harness the power of 'free'. A small freebie, a little 'emotional
  free sample', an act of generosity from your brand – these things
  are powerful.
- o Leave the door open creatively for the 'magic' in production. Don't
  slavishly shoot 'validated storyboards' (the Smash Martians falling over
  laughing was an 'accident').
- o Make sure 'over-rationalising' research doesn't iron these details out.
- o Where possible, test products and ideas on actual behaviour under
  real market conditions. These effects are hard to predict
  in advance.

STOP MAKING SENSE
THE WORK OF JOHN WEBSTER

Useful advice

No-one created more famous, well-loved advertising characters than UK creative John Webster. The Smash Martians. The Sugar Puffs Honey Monster. The Humphries. The Hofmeister and Cresta bears. The Kia Ora crow. All were 'distinctive'. None particularly 'made sense'.

There's a lovely story told about the time when Webster presented his new idea for Cresta, a frothy soft drink. The hero was a sunglasses-wearing cartoon polar bear who drawled 'It's Frothy Man!' when he swigged his Cresta. When Webster finished presenting the idea for the first time, the Cresta marketing director, somewhat bemused, asked, 'But why's there a polar bear in it?' 'Why not?' shrugged Webster. There was no answer to that.

Those of us raised on the mantra that ads need to be 'relevant' as well as distinctive might have sympathised with this client's concern. But Webster's work (and many highly effective campaigns since) reveals that we overvalue making sense in creative ideas. Often there's nothing intrinsically interesting and 'relevant' to say about our brands. This doesn't matter at all. People are more than happy for ads to playfully not 'make sense' – the liberating and happy upside of real people not caring about brands anything like as much as we think they do.

Notes:

_____

_____

_____

_____

_____

_____

_____

_____

HOW ~~NOT~~ TO BE DIFFERENT

'Rather than striving for meaningful perceived differentiation, marketers
should seek meaningless distinctiveness.
Branding lasts. Differentiation doesn't'
Byron Sharp

High on the received best practice checklist for many marketers is that successful communication must say something 'differentiated'. Cue time and effort spent reviewing what competitors 'say', worrying if competitors could say the same thing, researching to find something to say that's 'relevant' *and* 'differentiated', and testing propositions to make sure they're 'unique'.

Nothing wrong with all that, you might think. Surely brands do need to stand out from their competitors? Well, yes and no.

Standing out and being different is important for any brand. But don't confuse saying something different with saying something in a different way. Difference is less important than distinctiveness. A distinctive piece of communication on a category benefit will usually be more effective than a bland piece of communication on a differentiated positioning. But by and large, clients worry a lot when faced with the former, and don't mind much at all about the latter. But analysis of the IPA Databank suggests that, while branding is key to long-term profit, campaigns focusing on differentiation underperform.

This is consistent with other evidence that campaigns focusing on product messages tend to be less effective than those evoking emotional responses. It's also consistent with decades of research by the Ehrenberg-Bass

Institute, showing successful brands don't tend to be differentiated from competitors.

A cursory think about many famous, successful campaigns confirms this must be true. For over 20 years, Walkers crisps' campaign has won many creative and effectiveness awards. Multiple ads featuring Gary Lineker (famous ex-footballer nice guy) worked off the same basic proposition: Walkers crisps are irresistible. Irresistibility must be one of the most common propositions in food advertising. But Walkers showed that while often there may not be much to say about crisps that's genuinely different, you *can* talk about them in a distinctive way. This is what gets the tills ringing and bottom line growing. (Old Spice aftershave understands this too. 'Old Spice makes men smell nice' is not especially distinctive. But it's said in a wonderfully original way.)

Fail to understand this and you end up scrabbling around to find something… anything… different to say about your brand. As a result, you may end up missing more important category benefits, which are why the greatest number of people choose you.

We remember a senior Mars marketer ruing his decision to focus communication on an obscure dog food flavour just because it was unique – missing the fact it may have been unique because not many people wanted to buy it. Witness too all those haircare brands banging on about organo-peptides or other 'unique' pseudoscience benefits. But doing so in ads which seem identical to everyone else's.

So don't focus on saying something different. Instead, think about how you can *say something differently*. And if, after a creative presentation, a marketing director asks, 'But doesn't everyone say that in that way?', then perhaps you do need to think again.

DISTINCTIVENESS VS DIFFERENTIATION

2 minute checklist

o   If your brand is genuinely better or
     cheaper than the competition, then shout it
     from the rooftops.

o   But don't worry if you don't have a 'Unique Selling
     Point' (USP). Brands don't need to be different in functional,
     rational ways.

o   Aim for the heart of the market, not some obscure niche.

o   Don't shy away from the generic. Tapping into generic category
     values works (eg Tango Orange hit, Heineken refreshment).

o   Be distinctive, not different. Everything your brand does should
     have its own style and personality.

o   Don't worry about meaning and function. Some of the best distinctive
     assets are 'meaningless': the hole in Polo mints, or Pears soap's
     transparent amber colour.

o   Recognise the importance of distinctive assets *linked to your brand*:
     design, typeface, colours, logo, theme tunes, characters etc.

o   Make sure you know what your brand's distinctive 'memory structures' are.

o   Agree them. Codify them. Rigorously police them. Make
     everyone aware of them. Use them. Keep them consistent.

o   Think carefully before you mess with them.

BEING DISTINCTIVE
COMPARETHEMARKET

Useful case study

Launched in 2006, comparethemarket.com was a price comparison website focusing on car insurance – not exactly 'high interest'. It was also late to market, had no clear point of differentiation, and was outspent by its main rivals. The brand name was a problem too – generic and unmemorable.

Competitor advertising all looked the same. Ironically, because all brands were increasingly focusing on 'differentiating' claims in advertising, all the sites increasingly blended into one. Every brand's facts and benefits seemed the same. All ads showed computer screens, 'cars with stars' and price-saving claims. People weren't really listening. How were they to know if one claim was better than another?

So, inspired by what 'Gorilla' had done for Cadbury, comparethemarket took a different approach. Leave behind all the rational stuff. Do something distinctive. Make it utterly memorable. And don't worry if yes, frankly, it is a bit bonkers. Enter comparethemeerkat.com, headed by Aleksandr Orlov, the lovably eccentric Russian meerkat. And the rest is history. The campaign achieved all its 12 month objectives in just nine weeks. It became the number 1 brand for spontaneous awareness and consideration. Quote volumes rose by 83%. Cost per visit fell by 73%. Aleksandr became the first UK advertising property to have his own highly successful Twitter account. And, apparently, his 2010 'autobiography' generated more pre-orders than Tony Blair's memoirs, released at the same time… Be distinctive. Not different.

HOW ~~NOT~~ TO GET PEOPLE THINKING

'People dance with brands fleetingly'
Wendy Gordon

Sometimes when putting together pitch submissions, we're asked which brands exemplify best practice. Which brands do we admire for innovative marketing? Or for their social responsibility programmes?

Recently, the question was: 'Which brands are "thought leaders"?' We knew what sorts of brands they were alluding to: Apple, Google or Nike. And these brands certainly have a huge influence on marketers.

But the clients asking the question weren't just thinking about the marketing community. They meant which brands were 'thought leaders' in the wider world. And that got us thinking. Our conclusion? As far as real people are concerned, brands are almost without exception not 'thought leaders' at all.

We used to run a panel at our agency called 'Grapevine'. The idea was that we'd talk to cab drivers, hairdressers and pub owners to find out what people were talking about in their day-to-day lives. We'd hoped to let our clients know which brands were 'hot on the street': discussed and debated, or looked up to. Which were 'thought leaders' even?

After a number of these panel sessions, we had to admit failure. Real people weren't talking about brands at all. In the real world, brands don't even inspire thought – let alone lead it.

Online data confirms this. There's a lot of noise nowadays about the number of Facebook fans brands get. But the more interesting story is how small these numbers really are. In general, less than 1%

of users can be bothered to befriend their brand on Facebook (usually just to claim a discount). And less than 1% of these 'fans' ever post anything about the brand. That makes perfect sense. Real people have more important things to think and talk about than brands. In fact, we often forget that the main reason people choose brands is so they *don't* have to think. Brands offer mental shortcuts that make purchase decisions quicker and easier.

This was illustrated wonderfully in a brain scan experiment we saw. The study compared the brain activity of someone choosing between a leading brand and a weaker, lesser-known brand. Contrary to what we expected, there was *less* activity going on for the strong brand than the 'weaker' brand – strong brands are literally no-brainers. That's why they're strong.

Interestingly, there's also evidence that strong brands don't get talked about much either. When we analyse social media data for the car market, we find that the cars people talk about have the smallest market share – because they're the 'dream cars' most people will never be able to afford. The really successful brands that people actually buy generate far less 'buzz'.

There are some exceptions to this. Every brand has a small core of fanatics who think and talk about it: fashionistas who lust after Prada or music fans obsessed with their band. But these are minor exceptions. As Sharp points out, brand enthusiasts are a tiny minority. And generally, they're economically unimportant.

More importantly, there are occasions when a brand's marketing gets people thinking – and talking. It's a hard trick to pull off. But if you *can* get people down the pub saying, 'Have you seen that ad?', then it does seem to pay dividends. But to try to be a 'thought leader' on some higher level is usually over-ambitious. At least for commercial brands. It smacks of arrogance, and can be counterproductive – think of Benetton years ago.

At the end of a painfully long debate about a biscuit brand's positioning, a planner muttered, 'For God's sake, it's only a bloody biscuit!' She was right. Brands are useful. And they can be very profitable. But they're peripheral to real people's lives. Forget 'thought leadership'. Mostly it is only a biscuit. And we'll do more effective work if we remember this.

THOUGHT LEADERSHIP

2 minute checklist

o Remember: people don't have the
time, headspace or inclination to think about
most purchase decisions. Brands simplify the process,
so people *don't* have to think.

o Be wary about making people think. They don't like it, and
won't thank you for it.

o Make your brand quick, seamless and automatic to choose.
Literally be a no-brainer.

o Aim for 'mental availability': come to mind quickly and easily when
people consider the category, before other brands.

o Create strong, positive associations that make people warm towards
your brand. Emotion matters more than messages here.

o Use distinctive brand assets (from pack design to characters)
consistently so people identify your brand quickly *without* thinking.

o Closer to point of purchase, give information and help if people
want it.

o But don't intrude unnecessarily. People don't want to 'engage'
with brands.

o   Away from point of purchase, they're even less likely to think about you. So use things they *are* interested in to get their attention: stories, music, celebrities etc.

o   Brave advertising can be genuinely thought-provoking. Brands such as Dove and Always have challenged conventional thinking about beauty and women.

o   Get it right, and this is highly effective. Tapping into emotive issues can make your brand famous, and well-liked.

o   But trying to be a 'thought leader' is risky. It can seem cynical and opportunistic, and may backfire.

o   If you want to change the world, start from within. Walk the walk before you start talking the talk.

HOW ~~NOT~~ TO HAVE A RELATIONSHIP WITH YOUR CUSTOMERS

'Most of us go through life finding it hard enough to have good relationships with the real people in our life, let alone all the brands we buy'
Mars CMO

We were chatting with a marketing academic about marketing in the future. 'Of course,' he said, 'brands need to move away from mass marketing to having deeper personal relationships with their buyers.'

This bollocks talk is everywhere. Words like 'love', 'passion' and 'loyalty' litter social media briefs and brand plans. It's not enough for people to buy our products: we want 'relationships' with them. A lot of this talk is metaphorical. But too many people take the relationship analogy literally. That's not just nonsense. It's dangerous nonsense.

Think about brand relationships from the consumer perspective. It's a myth to believe we can take words like 'love' and 'passion' from human relationships

and apply them to brands we use every day. Real human relationships, even shallow ones, take time, effort and brainpower to build and maintain. Some scientists believe the main reason humans developed big brains was to manage relationships. But there seems to be a cognitive limit to the number of relationships we can handle. Beyond about 150 ('Dunbar's Number') our brains cannot cope anymore.

That doesn't leave much headspace for brands. And think what Dunbar's Number means for 'relationship marketing'. If you want a real relationship with customers, you're going to have to assign one member of staff for every 150 customers. The numbers don't make sense. And don't think you can fake a relationship with clever software. Millions of years of evolution have given us exquisitely sensitive social radar. Experiments suggest that even young babies can distinguish between real and fake social interactions.

Contrary to marketing's 'relationship' desires, most of us want brands to make our lives a bit easier. Then get out of the way. Few people want real, human relationships with brands. When they do, they're usually seen as immature (teenagers obsessing over pop stars) or weird (people with Harley-Davidson tattoos).

It's true, many brands do have a few people who feel strongly about them. And we should make the most of their 'passion' (by mobilising them to submit product ideas, or blog positively, even come up with communication ideas). But these brand 'lovers' will always be the exception, and rarely contribute much to the bottom line. Even for cult brands.

This 'relationship myth' isn't just harmless fantasy. The danger is our desire to create strong brand relationships distorts what smart marketing is really about. Research shows that brands become big and profitable by building weak relationships with lots of people. We know that when budgets are diverted from building penetration to building deeper relationships with fewer customers, profitability suffers. It's just not economically viable to have deep personal relationships with all your cat food buyers.

It's often assumed that the weakness of these many ties represents marketing failure. In fact, this is what people want. They don't want brands to be their friends. People love their cats. Not your cat food brand.

There are areas of marketing where strong personal relationships *do* play a crucial role. It makes sense to spend time and effort building close bonds with important suppliers, distributors, designers, regulators and journalists. But the main job of consumer marketing isn't to build a few strong ties – it's to build lots of weak ones.

Brands should aim to be more Jeeves-like servant than friend or lover. Mostly, we like our brands attentive, charming and helpful when required, but otherwise to be discreet. Then we can get on with the relationships that do matter to us: the ones we have with each other.

BRAND RELATIONSHIPS

2 minute checklist

o   Remember: having 'relationships' with brands is just an analogy. Brand relationships are not like human ones.

o   Don't expect a deep relationship. Buying thousands of brands a year means we can't devote headspace to them.

o   Don't expect people to think about, or spend time with, your brand. Brands save thinking and time, leaving us free to do other more important things.

o   Don't assume people know or care about you. We've only the fuzziest idea of a brand's provenance, offering and values. 'Personality' may be just 'the blue one'.

o   View weak brand relationships as a strength not a problem. Brands grow through weak relationships with the many, not deep relationships with the few.

o   So don't waste time trying to build relationships with customers, unless you're a salesman or account manager (with fewer than 150 of them).

o   Focus on penetration, not loyalty. Build preferences and habits, not 'relationships'.

o   Don't try to be 'friends' with brand buyers. Be more Jeeves. Understand and anticipate needs. Serve them when needed. Then keep out of the way.

Notes:

_____

_____

_____

_____

_____

_____

_____

_____

WHAT ~~NOT~~ TO SAY

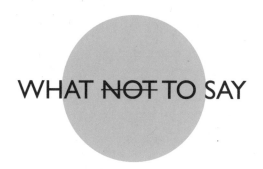

'People will forget what you said. People will forget what you did. But people will never forget how you made them feel'
Maya Angelou

In 2010, the formation of the first post-war coalition government in the UK was preceded by something new in British election campaigning: televised 'Leaders' Debates'. These were billed as an historic opportunity for the public to watch the three party leaders debate head to head, supposedly giving us a clearer idea of candidates' policy, and information on which to base voting.

So it's interesting to note how the commentary on these debates hardly focused on the candidates' policies or messages at all. Instead, the most 'persuasive' bits, the 'reasons to believe' in one leader over another, had far more to do with the way one addressed audience members by their first name, or another talked to viewers by addressing the camera. The 'soft', non-verbal

communication people received from the candidates seemed more influential in decision making than the 'hard', verbal messages.

For anyone familiar with the work of psychologist Paul Watzlawick, this is no surprise. Watzlawick argued that 'meta-communication' (ie non-verbal things such as tone of voice, body language and facial expressions) is much more influential in relationship building than 'communication' (messages and supporting evidence). *What* you say matters less than *how* you say it.

The TV debates in America between Nixon and Kennedy proved this meta-communication power more than 50 years ago. Voters who heard the 1960 debates on the radio were sure Nixon had the best arguments. But those who saw it on TV were more swayed by the contrast between Kennedy's healthy tan and Nixon's sweaty pallor. And TV decided the election.

In the commercial world, we're still in thrall to the 'message myth'. Our creative briefs, concept tests, pre-tests and tracking research all assume that a message is vital in 'persuading' people to buy one brand vs another. So we spend vast amounts of time and money testing propositions, and researching message cut-through and recall.

Yet research based on the IPA Databank suggests that our obsession with product messages is wrong. Campaigns containing little or no product, but working instead by appealing to emotions or 'herd instincts' (the two usually go together), are twice as effective as conventional 'message' advertising. It seems that in marketing, like politics, meta-communication is what matters.

A fascinating example of meta-communication power comes from a Philips electric shaver campaign we worked on. Shaver advertising usually focuses on rational product benefits.

And Philips' previous advertising was no exception. But a Philips TV ad for its 'Moisturizing Shaving System' was the complete opposite. No voiceover. No product information. No rational message at all. Just a sensual, dreamlike sci-fi fantasy, accompanied by enigmatic music. Not surprisingly, the ad performed well below norms for 'communication' in tracking. But sales effects were remarkable. Market share doubled in six months. Evidence from brain scanning suggested that key to that success was the powerful emotional response the ad evoked in men. This had a bigger effect on long-term memory and sales than any 'persuasive' product messages.

It seems that we should pay less attention to the content of advertising, and far more to 'softer' aspects of communication – such as casting, soundtrack and choice of director.

Our message? You don't always need one.

BRAND MESSAGES

2 minute checklist

o   Ask yourself, are you building long-term
    brand equity, delivering short-term responses
    (activation) or both (brand response)?

o   If brand building, focus on emotions, feelings and
    associations. This influences people even when they're not
    interested in buying. And has long-lasting effects.

o   Focus less on messages for brand activity. Emotional priming is
    better than rational persuasion.

o   For activation, it's the reverse. Messages work well, especially if they
    are a 'reason to buy now', such as a special offer.

o   Make it easy for people to find information to make the final purchase
    decision: prices, product specifications, contact details etc.

o   And make it easy to buy. Include a direct response mechanism if you can.

o   Integrate brand and activation, so one reminds people of the other.

o   But don't try too hard to entertain or seduce for activation.
    Just get on with selling.

o   If you're trying to do brand and activation together, consider splitting
    the jobs. Rational selling messages may dilute emotional power.
    Entertaining people in active shopping mode can irritate.

o   Best often to do the two jobs separately;
    with different targeting, in different media.

o   Messages work best for activation, but sometimes
    there's a role for a message in brand ads too.

o   Shout about a genuinely world-beating USP that real people
    will be interested in. But remember, this is rare.

o   Use 'reasons to buy' as 'functional alibis', so people can justify
    brand choice. (Car ads may talk about engineering, allowing us to
    post-rationalise feelings about ownership.)

o   Use concrete facts to generate feelings, even if they aren't the main
    message. A little 'truth' can symbolise brand values, or be a jumping-off
    point for an emotional story.

o   Consider using brand facts as 'meaningless distinctives'. Even if not
    functionally relevant.

o   Don't get hung up on a 'single-minded proposition'. Brand ads may
    need no message at all. They may 'say' many things implicitly.
    Activation may communicate detailed information, not a single
    'reason to buy'.

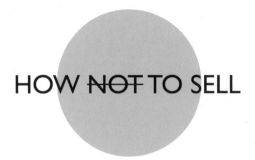

HOW ~~NOT~~ TO SELL

'We should never forget we're the uninvited guest in the living room'
Martin Boase

The death in 2015 of 92-year-old Olive Cooke, Britain's oldest British Legion charity poppy seller, highlighted a dark side of our business we rarely confront. After allegations that Mrs Cooke was 'hounded to death' by charities begging for money, the press raged about unscrupulous fundraisers. The Prime Minister promised tough action to protect the vulnerable.

Regardless of the circumstances of Mrs Cooke's tragic death, public hostility to some companies' more strident activity is clearly real. Everyone has a story about annoying fundraising techniques. Mumsnet has over 6,000 threads devoted to them. According to the Fundraising Standards Board (FRSB), complaints about fundraising increased by 55% in the two years up to Mrs Cooke's death.

Google data is revealing. Start typing 'charities are' and Google suggestions based on the most popular search terms are 'scams', 'businesses', 'corrupt' and so on. So why do people find charity marketing so annoying?

Partly, it's a question of volume. According to the FRSB, in 2014 Britons were exposed to over 20 billion fundraising messages. More important is the way those messages are targeted. Charities have become notorious exponents of the 'loyalty' approach to marketing. This says that the easiest way to make money is to screw more of it out of existing customers. Give money to a charity, and requests immediately follow. The more you give, the more you're asked for. Little wonder people like poor Mrs Cooke feel 'hounded'.

Charities are not alone in this. A recent order for a Christmas gift online for a niece prompted the company to email every day since purchase, in the misguided belief that this would keep us 'loyal'.

Intrusive media are another source of anger. The harder a channel is to ignore, the more virulent the reaction. With telesales and paid street fundraisers ('chuggers') at the top of the list. But their intrusiveness is the very attraction to users. To fundraisers, they work. Maybe they do generate short-term cash, but what's the long-term brand effect? Nobody knows. Because nobody measures it.

Again, charities are not alone in being blind to negative effects of marketing. We once worked on a leading credit card. It had 5 million users who were mailed a monthly statement. Keen to maximise return on mailing costs, the brand printed an 'offer' every month on the envelope flap. A whole department was dedicated to finding items to sell in this way – from nasal hair clippers to thigh-firming devices.

Response rates were very low (less than 1%), but still high enough to make money. The client seemed surprised when we asked what the 99% of *non-responders* felt about these tacky offers. Surely they cheapened the bank's professional reputation? They didn't know. They'd never asked. But one customer *we* asked likened the practice to 'going to see your bank manager and them standing up and trying to flog you the chair they're sitting on'.

One factor behind this might be measurement. The direct, short-term benefits of hard-sell marketing techniques are easy to measure (and indeed easy to overestimate). But the long-term brand damage they can do among the silently fuming majority is easier to ignore. And may not be apparent until too late.

Market research doesn't give enough weight to these issues. Less time measuring 'brand loyalty' and 'brand love', and a bit more attention to 'brand annoyance', would benefit us all.

HOW TO SELL WITHOUT ANNOYING PEOPLE

2 minute checklist

o   Remember: your competition isn't other brands, it's people's lives. People don't want to give you their attention.

o   If you're not interesting, entertaining or useful, you're an irritating distraction. At best, people will screen you out. At worst, they'll resent you for it.

o   So don't *demand* attention. People find intrusive marketing annoying, and that can do long-term damage to your brand.

o   Don't sacrifice long-term goodwill for short-term gain. Marketing appearing effective in the short term can lose you money long term.

o   Don't be fooled by short-term response measures. Think how all the people who *didn't* respond might be feeling.

o   Think from the other end of the telescope. What are people doing? People watch TV for relaxation, so shouty, hard-sell ads aren't welcome. People looking for information online may not want to be entertained.

o   Take particular care with highly targeted activity. Talk to people directly, and they expect you to understand them individually. Don't get their name wrong.

o   Don't use excessive frequency. It's better to
    talk to many people once than annoy the same
    people repeatedly. Use digital techniques to cap frequency.

o   Be wary of 'loyalty' strategies extracting value from the same
    people. It leads to a shrinking pool of irritated customers.

o   Be a 'pull' not 'push' brand. If people feel good about you,
    you have permission to sell to them. Build a strong brand and
    response rates will rise.

o   Spend around 60% of your communication budget on long-term
    brand building. And 40% on short-term activation.

o   Remember: excessive activation damages brands. Too many
    promotions make you look cheap. And nobody likes spam.

Notes:

_____

_____

_____

_____

_____

_____

_____

_____

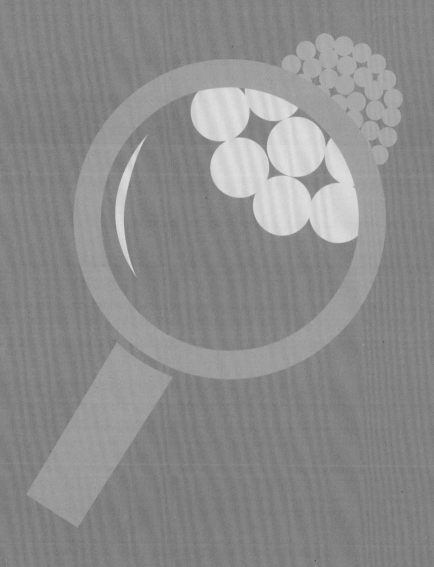

RESEARCH AND ANALYSIS

'What seems to have gone wrong is that people have said one thing and then they did something else in the ballot box'

Peter Kellner, YouGov

FOUR

INTRODUCTION

Research, in all its many forms, is the raw material we planners work with. The clay we throw onto the planning potter's wheel to shape our strategies. Clearly, whole books could be devoted to research. And many good ones have. This chapter, then, is not an exhaustive 'how to do it' guide to qualitative or quantitative research techniques.

Instead, here we step back and look more broadly at some important principles of research. And based on these principles, we offer thoughts and tips on how to use research more usefully.

In the first article we discuss where to use research, and what sort of research is best. And when to back off and not research. In the next two articles we remind ourselves of the power of qualitative research done well – yes, even the much disparaged 'focus group'.

The remaining four articles look at some of the many ways research numbers are routinely used and abused in strategy thinking: too many numbers used where it doesn't matter, and not enough numbers used where it does. Big numbers used without context. Bad numbers generated from bad research thinking. And comparative numbers viewed in misleading ways.

All resulting in flawed strategies and ineffective ads.

WHEN ~~NOT~~ TO BE RIGOROUS

*'Logic and over-analysis can immobilize and sterilize an idea. It's like love —
the more you analyze it, the faster it disappears'*
Bill Bernbach

A few years ago, we were discussing a brief. Looking back on it, the team were frustrated at where it had gone wrong. The strategy was great. The creative team had an idea. And everyone thought this would work brilliantly. But then someone did some quick calculations. This revealed that, to meet sales targets, we'd need to double the number of users. It was clear the campaign could never deliver this, and it was too late to come up with anything else.

So while the account team were honing the nuances of the creative idea, they'd failed to look at the numbers that mattered. This 'misplaced rigour syndrome' comes in two forms: too much rigour where you don't need it, and not enough where you do.

There are times when we do need rigour — lots of it. Long before going anywhere near creative teams, it's vital to know whether the campaign is capable of working. How many people does it need to reach? What behaviour does it need to change? By how much? And how much profit will that deliver?

The IPA Databank shows that setting clear business objectives can quadruple effectiveness. But too often this due diligence is left to the last minute. By which time it's too late to change course.

Rigour is vital at the back-end too — after the campaign has run. Did the campaign work? How big were its effects? Was it profitable? The IPA data shows that clients and agencies who regularly evaluate in hard business terms achieve much better results, because they learn what really works.

Unfortunately, this rigorous post-campaign evaluation rarely happens either. Getting hold of sales data and analysing it properly is too much like hard work (unless there's an Effectiveness Award to be won). Easier to look at a few proxy measures – Facebook likes or YouTube hits – and move on.

The problem with this casual approach is that, without proper evidence-based feedback, clients and agencies can lose their instinct for effectiveness. It's not unknown for a campaign to be lauded as an example of cutting-edge thinking, only for sales data to reveal it was an expensive turkey.

But nowadays, if there's too little rigour at the start and end of the advertising process, there's generally far too much so-called rigour in the middle. So instead of looking at sales data, we get over-intellectualised analysis of propositions, message rankings and brand hierarchies.

Clients love intermediate measures of all kinds. Even if they have no correlation with business success, because they offer the false promise of easy decision making. We recently sat through a 60-chart quantitative pre-test debrief. Even with two charts of analysis for every second of the ad, we were still no wiser as to how the ad would perform in the real world. Good old-fashioned intuition, honed by experience, would have been a more reliable guide. But that would have required us all to use some judgement.

So what do we recommend? Well, a freer approach to the creative process, counterbalanced by a more rigorous approach to objective setting and evaluation. Interestingly, that's what smarter marketing companies seem to be moving towards. Especially in the digital space, where it's often cheaper to experiment. As marketing strategists Leslie Moeller and Edward Landry put it: 'Be creative and measure what happens. If it works, do more of it. If it doesn't work, go back and be creative again.'

Try it. You might be surprised.

WHEN TO BE RIGOROUS

2 minute checklist

o   Understand where you need numbers
     and where you don't.

o   Use numbers when you're setting objectives and
     planning media. This bit needs to be rigorous.

o   Set clear targets for business results (sales, revenue and
     profit) and consumer behaviour (eg penetration, frequency
     of purchase).

o   Check that your numbers stack up. Will the behavioural effects
     deliver enough sales and profit?

o   Look at previous campaigns in this category. Are your targets realistic?

o   Think about what a discount will do to margins. Remember: most
     promotions are unprofitable.

o   Be wary of loyalty strategies. Remember: sales are primarily driven by
     penetration, not loyalty.

o   Check the reach of your activity. Conversion rates are always low
     (~0.1% for online display), so aim to reach many more people than
     you need to recruit.

o   Check that your budget is big enough.
     Use Share of Voice (SOV) analysis if you can.

- o Evaluate campaign results rigorously.
      Compare behaviour and sales against targets.
      Did your campaign deliver?
- o Use controlled tests or econometric modelling to isolate
      the incremental effects of your campaign.
- o Learn from everything you do. Find out what works and
      makes money. Then do more of it.
- o Pay less attention to 'intermediate measures', like ad awareness or
      'engagement'. There is no clear and simple relationship between
      these metrics and sales.
- o Don't rely just on intermediate measures to judge campaigns.
- o Campaigns with low ad awareness can deliver great sales results.
      Campaigns with great tracking scores can bomb.
- o Use qualitative as well as quantitative research. Pay more attention
      to sales than tracking. And always use your judgement.

RIGOUR
WALL'S ICE CREAM

Useful case study

The 2016 Wall's 'Talking Ice Cream' campaign is a good example of 'back-end' rigour, in this case, rigorous analysis of the sales effectiveness of different media. Something not often done... because it's hard to compare media 'apples with apples'.

During the summer of 2016, econometrics showed that Wall's sold 2.7 million extra ice creams as a result of their new campaign. The campaign ran on mobile, Twitter, Facebook and Outdoor (posters on bus-sides and on the streets). A flurry of different measures was reported by media after the campaign had run, but without a 'common currency' it was impossible to work out which media had done what.

With a bit of digging we were able to produce the numbers we needed. First, we worked out the number of impressions each media generated. This meant we could then calculate cost/impression by channel.

Then we could relate this to the sales contribution by channel we had worked out from econometrics. We learnt a number of lessons:

	Impressions	Media cost	Cost per impression
Mobile	1.4m	£215,000	£0.153
Twitter	6.6m	£69,057	£0.010
Outdoor	458.0m	£1,583,000	£0.003
Facebook	154.0m	£199,050	£0.001
Other	28.0m	£364,000	£0.013
TOTAL	648.0m	£2,430,107	£0.004

Source: Mindshare, Kinetic, Unilever

- Outdoor was the most effective medium, but Facebook was more efficient – achieving almost as many sales on a lower spend. The two worked in synergy.

- Exposure (ie number of impressions by channel) was the single biggest factor driving effectiveness. Outdoor dominated in terms of exposure, followed by Facebook.

- We can all get excited by new media opportunities. But here was a timely reminder that Twitter impressions were tiny compared with Outdoor and Facebook. *Just one week of London bus-sides delivered more impressions than three months of Twitter.*

The lesson here is the value of rigour when analysing and evaluating media. Only by putting numbers in context and creating a common currency could channels be meaningfully compared.

HOW ~~NOT~~ TO USE FOCUS GROUPS

'The problem with market research is that people don't think how they feel, they don't say what they think and they don't do what they say'
David Ogilvy

Many years ago, in the early 1990s, we were working on repositioning a global whisky brand. This required us to attend qualitative research in New York and Los Angeles. Trained in the art of conducting what we quaintly used to call 'group discussions', we were stunned at what confronted us. In the UK at that time, groups were always convened in real people's houses, and were rarely attended by clients. A common sense and trusting approach to recruitment and discussion guides prevailed. Time was protected to analyse and interpret fieldwork before the debrief.

In our US whisky 'focus groups', things were very different. The research took place in beige, faux boardroom settings – usually around a large table. A pack of clients sat behind a one-way mirror – chatting loudly, ridiculing respondents' ignorance of their brand, and paying more attention to the takeaway menu than the proceedings. The moderator had little role really, beyond putting a prepared list of questions in a set order to the bored respondents. After a cursory chat with the moderator at the end, the clients each went away with their own idea of the research findings. Back then, this seemed a travesty: a pathetic distortion of the true principles of qualitative research.

But today, this experience is becoming the norm. Here are a few situations we've encountered recently. Crazy requirements to recruit respondents according to a complicated client segmentation involving lists of 30 statements and 9-point scales. Weeks spent signing off a 7-page discussion guide, with numerous clients involved in changing odd words on it, so 'everyone is aligned'. Clients flying to the US for just two groups, arriving halfway through the first and chatting through the second. Marketing teams spending weeks micro-managing every aspect of the research process before the fieldwork, then demanding instant debriefs straight after the groups finished. That's before we start on the issue of live streaming, where weary clients in their pyjamas log in and out during research in the small hours on the other side of the world, adding comments to the text box and communicating with colleagues during the research.

It's almost de rigeur to bash focus groups these days. They're old-fashioned. You don't get anything new or different from them. The problem, though, is not with the focus groups. It's the way we use them.

Expertly practised groups can give us a uniquely sensitive understanding of people's relationships with brands and communication. They're probably still the best means at our disposal of accessing 'System 1' thinking: the emotional, implicit, non-verbal thought processes which drive most buying behaviour. The silences, the arm crossing, the raised eyebrow. The words *not* chosen. The laughter, the leaning forward or leaning back. The change in group energy level – all these are more potent indicators of what's really going on in people's minds than the words they use.

The trouble is that focus groups are increasingly interpreted by clients at 'System 2' level: the realm of the verbal, logical and post-rationalised. One step removed from respondents on the other side of the glass, clients concentrate just on the verbal content of the discussion. Ask yourself, if you're being tried by a jury, would you rather they were in the room with you? Or in their pyjamas at 2am half watching a small screen on the other side of the world?

Through our industry's well-intentioned effort to make focus groups more 'rigorous' and 'scientific', we've neutered and distorted them so they no longer deliver the thing they were designed for: sensitive and empathic understanding of other people's perspectives. The result? At best they're less useful. At worst, they're downright misleading. If focus groups no longer work for you, is it the technique? Or the way you're using them?

HOW TO USE FOCUS GROUPS

2 minute checklist

o   Don't dismiss focus groups. Done well, they're
    still very useful.
o   Make sure you understand what good qualitative
    research looks like, and how to get it. It's easy to do badly.
o   Choose your qualitative researcher carefully, especially for
    research in a different culture or language.
o   Choose the person, not the company. Malcolm Gladwell's 10,000
    hours' experience 'rule' is a good guide. Get recommendations.
o   Beware clients holding their own 'insight sessions' with 'consumers'. It's
    useful up to a point. But it's not the same thing as employing a trained,
    experienced researcher.
o   Don't over-complicate the recruitment criteria. Save that for
    quantitative surveys.
o   Don't ask qualitative research to tell you things other data does better
    (eg tracking product usage).
o   Don't just listen to what people say. Pay attention to *how* they say it
    and what they *don't* say. Look out for 'the dogs that don't bark in
    the night'. Good researchers know this. Clients don't.

o   Always fight for time for your researcher to
do proper analysis. If you deny your researcher this,
you're denying yourself quality research. Simply watching
the groups is *not* enough.

o   Don't waste time noodling over the discussion guide. Give
that time to your researcher for analysis.

o   Do spend enough time getting good stimulus for creative ideas
(we never spend enough time on this bit).

o   Use other research techniques too – eg social listening, ethnography
or your own good old observation etc. But focus groups done well
will always be a planner's friend.

o   Use qualitative and quantitative research in synergy. Focus groups help
make sense of data; data helps test hypotheses coming out
of qualitative.

HOW ~~NOT~~ TO THINK ABOUT 'POSITIVE' RESPONSES

'I wanted "The Office" to be a million people's favourite show, not 10 million people's 10th favourite show'
Ricky Gervais

We came across something unusual the other day: two words not often heard together, but two words that reminded us of a myth about positive response.

The scene was a research debrief. Two alternative ad ideas for a dessert brand had been explored in qualitative research. It was a tricky bit of research to interpret. The ideas were new. The two alternative routes were very different. And the stimulus material was quite basic.

One idea featured vignettes of different people enjoying the brand in everyday scenarios, set to a great soundtrack. Everyone said they liked this one in the groups. The other idea featured a darker, tongue-in-cheek depiction of the lengths a character would go to enjoy this brand of desserts. A few people loved this route. Others didn't like it at all.

This is a research scenario which can easily lead to literal and flawed recommendations. Luckily, the researcher was an experienced pair of hands. He acknowledged the uniformly positive response to the vignettes route. But then he described this response with two words – 'false positive' – and recommended instead going with the polarising route.

We loved that phrase 'false positive'. Because positive responses in research aren't always what they seem. Failing to spot this can easily distort the evaluation of ideas.

People in qualitative research are generally pretty polite. They tend to default to the familiar. And they tend to look for similarity, not difference. All this produces a number of politely rationalised positive responses, which only experienced researchers are alert to as warning signs: 'the children would like that'; 'they're showing there's something for everyone'; and the red-light comment for all new products – 'it would be good for camping'.

Like respondents in research, researchers can also be understandably eager to please. For many years, pre-testing research has been criticised (often unfairly) for killing off early creative ideas by failing to understand the phenomenon of 'false negatives'. These are negative comments that aren't really negative but result from common research scenarios. Unclear stimulus material. Misunderstandings of the idea. Or simply the new and unfamiliar (people generally prefer similar to change). But perhaps some researchers are now so wary of this false negative charge that they over-enthusiastically look for the positive instead. (As planners back at BMP, we researched all our creative ideas. New clients were often suspicious about this, until they realised we were much harsher on our own ideas than outside researchers.)

Perhaps now we've all become better

at recognising that 'negative' isn't always bad. But we're less good at realising that 'positive' isn't always good.

This matters. Because when researching anything new, a polarised strong response is often a more reliable predictor of success than a uniformly mild liking. People take time to take the new to their hearts. From successful British comedies such as *Fawlty Towers* and *Only Fools and Horses* (both of which were panned by many when they first ran), to the award-winning Marmite animal welfare spoof 'Neglect' campaign, strong new ideas tend to polarise. At least initially.

Failure to recognise this in research, and going instead with the mildly positive, must contribute to the high failure rate of new products. And to the lack-lustre performance of many ads. For the same reasons, we question the effectiveness of many vignette-style 'different users using the brand in different situations set to music' ads. These quasi-mood film ads undoubtedly get uniformly positive responses in pitches and research. What's not to like? But there's evidence to question their real-world effectiveness. 'A little bit for everyone' in research may mean 'not enough standout for anyone' in the real world.

HOW TO JUDGE POSITIVE AND NEGATIVE RESPONSES

2 minute checklist

o   Do pay attention to 'liking'. It's the best predictor
    of sales effectiveness (Advertising Research Foundation
    study, 1991).

o   But remember that liking is more complex than it seems.
    Legendary qualitative researcher Wendy Gordon talks about
    five kinds of liking ('ingenuity', 'meaningful', 'energetic', 'warmth' and
    'doesn't rub up the wrong way').

o   Don't judge ads solely on liking, or on any other single metric. There
    is no one silver bullet predictor.

o   Don't ask people directly about 'likes' and 'dislikes'. You're asking them
    to rationalise what are emotional responses.

o   Pay more attention to non-verbal liking cues: leaning forward, smiles,
    animated talking.

o   Consider newer, indirect ways of measuring liking, such as an 'Implicit
    Association Test' (IAT) and facial expression scales.

o   When you're asking people to judge your ads, look
    for the comparative 'anchor'. People tend to answer
    such questions in a comparative way, even if they're not
    aware of it.

o   Watch out for misleading responses. Comparing
    likeability of ideas in qualitative can give false positives.
    Is the 'winning' idea just the best of a bad bunch?

o   Remember: 'positive' responses aren't always good. Watch
    out for the polite, the similar and the inoffensive.

o   Don't be too afraid of polarised, or even 'negative', responses.
    They're a sign of energy. This is what you're looking for when
    researching creative work.

MISLEADING RESEARCH
M&S

Useful case study

Here's a cautionary tale of how 'humankind cannot bear too much reality' – especially in the world of women's fashion. Despite what people in research might say…

Back in 2000, M&S were facing a slump in sales. Brand appeal was declining. Women's clothing was key to turning this situation around. In an attempt to be brave and zig against the zag of women's fashion, M&S decided to celebrate the fit of their clothes – whatever women's shape and size.

Their new ad broke in the Autumn of that year. It didn't show any of the new M&S fashion range. In fact, it didn't showcase any clothes at all. But it did show a real, size 16 woman. In the now infamous ad we see the woman casting off clothing as she runs up a sun-drenched hill. On reaching the top, she stands naked, arms outstretched, proudly shouting 'I'm normal!' The voiceover tells us that M&S has conducted the largest ever survey of women's bodies, and, 'You'll be pleased to hear that if you're not average, you're normal'.

In groups, women loved it. They were fed up with seeing women advertising fashion brands who looked nothing like them, they said. It was a great idea to instead show 'someone just like them', they said. And with 68% recall soon after airing, the ad clearly made a big impression.

But sales in M&S women's fashion tanked. And the campaign was replaced the next year by a new, more conventional fashion campaign featuring a stellar line-up of models including Twiggy, Lizzie Jagger and Erin O'Connor. They were all wearing M&S new fashion lines. And they were all several sizes smaller than a size 16.

So be very careful when people say in research that they want to see people 'like them'. What they really want to see – especially in the world of fashion and beauty – is their 'Idealised Self': the person they *strive* to be. Them at their very best. Not the warts-and-all 'Actual Self' they see when they look in the full-length mirror.

Be careful with reality. And be careful with what people say in research. It might not be what they mean.

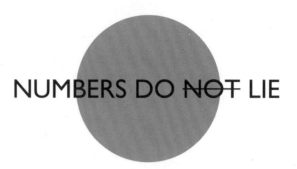

NUMBERS DO ~~NOT~~ LIE

'A simple fact, which the numerate people who predominate in advertising research never seem to grasp, is that numbers to the innumerate are seen as infallible'
Stanley Pollitt

The other day we did something we hadn't done for a while. A young client, new to quantitative testing, asked us to go through his pre-testing questionnaire for a proposed ad. Did it cover the issues he was interested in, he asked.

It was an illuminating exercise. Like most of us, we spend a lot of time in quantitative ad research debrief meetings. Lots of charts are perused. The numbers look scientific. Authoritative. Objective. But peer behind the curtain, and things look less impressive.

For a start, if this were real science, researchers would be trying to replicate real viewing conditions. But our questionnaire research scenario bore no resemblance to real-life watching.

The ad tested was an animatic, not a real ad, which respondents were asked to watch on their computer, alone and paying close attention to. Some were asked to film themselves on their webcams watching the ad – the mechanics of this making the situation even more odd, with respondents instructed on how to sit, arrange their hair and adjust lighting conditions.

Real people, meanwhile, watch ads in distracted, 'lean back' mode. Wearing onesies. Often eating and drinking. Alone or with friends and family. And if this were real science, there'd be some attempt to replicate real buying decision making in the questionnaire. This was an FMCG brand, where shoppers spend on average fewer than four seconds on each buying decision in-store. But with 60 questions to answer, this research interrogation would take far longer, the respondent no doubt bored witless by the end of it.

This matters a lot. Psychological research shows that people's choices and answers to questions are heavily dependent on how much time you give them. Ask for a quick answer and you'll get an intuitive 'System 1' response. Ask them a series of considered questions and you'll get a more rational 'System 2' response. A brilliant demonstration of this is the 'Wilson Spooner jam experiment'. Here, people were asked to taste a range of jams. Asked to decide quickly which jam they liked, ordinary people were just as good as food critics at picking good jam. But when asked detailed questions about sweetness, colour and so on, their intuitions were overridden. And they made poorer choices.

So, given our 'test ad' was for a product chosen quickly in an intuitive 'System 1' way, the long 'System 2' questionnaire may well give misleading feedback. Not least because of the nature of the questions asked. Many were 'standard' ones, meaning handy comparison with 'norms'. But our brand was unusual.

Many of the questions just didn't apply to it at all. Add in the fact that the questionnaire writer was obviously not a native English speaker, and the result was a tedious and baffling mess guaranteed to confuse and annoy the most patient of respondents. And that matters too.

When people are bored and annoyed by a questionnaire, they'll transfer those feelings to the brands and ads in question. So, even a quick glance at the questionnaire raised doubts about this research.

But who considers all this 'input' when presented with the spurious precision and certainty of the output. And it led to us to thinking how it's odd that clients and agency people often watch qualitative groups to listen to respondents 'first hand', but we don't remember anyone ever asking to experience quantitative research in action. And why are qualitative discussion guides more likely to be pored over than quantitative questionnaires?

It seems, to misquote Bismarck, numbers are like sausages – it's better not to see them being made.

ASSESSING NUMBERS

2 minute checklist

o Don't be bamboozled by numbers. Just
   because there's a number attached to it, doesn't
   meant it's a valid or relevant concept. Research
   numbers *may* indicate how people are thinking and feeling
   – or not.

o Don't just take research numbers at face value. Ask how those
   numbers were 'made'.

o Find out exactly what questions were asked, of whom, in what
   context. Remember: questionnaire responses are sensitive to
   changes in methodology, wording and ordering.

o Find out what stimuli were used. How were the questions administered?
   Who to? What's it like to be a respondent? Context matters a lot.

o Try answering the questions yourself. It's a real eye-opener.

o Beware long, boring or difficult questionnaires. People get fed up, and
   won't answer them reliably.

o   Don't trust responses too much. We don't
    understand our own thoughts, feelings or behaviour.
    And we all lie sometimes.
o   Remember: people answer questionnaires in a 'probabilistic'
    way. They usually try to answer questions, even if they can't
    really articulate what they feel. But ask them again, and you'll get
    different answers.
o   Use short, quick questions to stop people over-thinking. Or a
    technique like the IAT, which measures how *fast* people respond.
    Not just what they say.

HOW ~~NOT~~ TO SEE THE WOOD FOR THE TREES

'To see what is in front of one's nose needs a constant struggle'
George Orwell

Some years ago, we met a 'data insight' client who was excited about large customer data sets. 'It's the granularity that's so amazing,' he enthused. 'For instance, people who shop in petrol stations on a Thursday…' and so it went on. Eventually, we asked what was happening to market share. He seemed annoyed. Market share wasn't relevant for a complex business like his, he said. We analysed his data in a different way. Not drilling down into the detail, but aggregating up to find the trends. And we soon found patterns his data-mining techniques had missed. We found six important measures of market share. All were in long-term decline.

It's commonly assumed that the more data you have, the better. But in our experience, the more granular the data, the harder it is to see the wood for the trees. Digital data is often daily or hourly, making it easier to measure short-term marketing effects. But much harder to measure long-term effects. They get lost in the noise. Similarly, if you analyse sales by store and SKU (Stock-Keeping Unit), the effects of promotions seem huge. But brand-level data shows they're much smaller once cannibalisation and store switching are taken into account.

Those may sound pedantic points. But they can have big consequences.

When EPOS first gave us high-frequency, granular sales data in the late 1980s, the result was a big increase in price promotions, because the new data exaggerated their effects. We did learn that excessive promotion can erode long-term profits and commoditise whole categories – but not before the damage was done. Retailers did rather better than brand owners out of that, as the winner was often Own Label. But granular data doesn't always help them either.

We once asked a furniture retailer about year-on-year sales performance. 'I haven't got time for that,' he exclaimed. 'I want to know why I haven't sold any beds in Chester this morning!' Not surprisingly, his company went bust.

Granular customer data can be dangerously seductive. Too many brands obsess over fine segmentation and tight targeting, despite evidence that the real money comes from broad reach and high market share. And now we have digital data at the customer level. That makes it possible to customise selling messages with uncanny accuracy – as any Amazon shopper knows. And as online data evolves, our understanding of how marketing affects behaviour will deepen.

But analysing data at the individual level can't measure important 'herd effects', which only emerge at the group level.

And social media metrics won't help, because herd effects are mostly non-verbal and offline.

Finally, there's the problem of 'false positives'. The more things you measure, the more fluke results you get. So granular data often shows patterns that aren't really there.

Granular data does have uses, of course – particularly in the realm of sales activation. But it can be misleading when brand building, where effects are broad brush and long term. And that's where big profits lie.

So just as we need to balance short and long-term marketing strategies, so we should balance granular, bottom-up analysis with broader, top-down perspectives. That means designing data systems that allow us to shift easily from zoom to wide angle. It also means employing people who can see the big picture, not just the fine detail.

Get the balance wrong, and 'Big Data' will lead you dangerously astray. Get it right, and you can move from Big Data to Big Insights, Big Brands and Big Profits.

HOW TO GET A WORM'S-EYE AND A BIRD'S-EYE VIEW

2 minute checklist

o   Don't be too seduced by 'Big Data'. More detail doesn't always mean more insight.

o   Don't assume 'granular' data (individual store, customer, transaction) is better than 'aggregate' data (national or regional over weeks or months). Big Data can make it hard to see the wood for the trees.

o   Remember: granular data is usually short term. Short-term data exaggerates short-term effects (eg promotional spikes) and underestimates long-term effects (eg the damage promos do to profits).

o   So analyse long-term effects too. This usually requires a more top-level approach.

o   Always look at the *net* effect of activity, using both aggregate data and the detailed stuff. Keep the big picture in view.

o   Don't just rely on 'dashboards' to summarise top-level figures at a given point in time. Pay more attention to the big, macro *trends* that affect your brand.

o   Granular data is less useful for this trend analysis.
    you don't need 'Big Data', you need 'Long Data'.
o   Set up systems for collecting important top-level
    numbers over time. Remember: three years' data is the
    minimum needed for trend analysis.
o   Beware of spurious correlations from 'data mining': trawling for
    relationships between different variables. Test for statistical
    significance at a higher level of confidence when looking at
    multiple correlations.

BIG NUMBERS CANNOT FAIL TO IMPRESS

'Curiosity is bad for cats, but good for stats'
Tim Harford

In the next chapter we look at how sloppy language stops us thinking clearly. In this article we consider sloppy numbers. More specifically, the abuse of numbers by quoting them out of context.

Let's take a recent case study which made a big deal of the fact that the ad got 1.6 million views on YouTube. It sounds big and impressive. But is it really?

Faced with big numbers like this, it's a good idea to re-express them as percentages. A quick calculation suggests that those 1.6 million views represented just 3% of the target audience. And the true percentage is probably lower still, because some viewers will be outside the target audience. Some will live abroad. And some will view more than once.

Another useful sanity check is to compare numbers against costs. Looking at digital case studies, we're struck by how all flaunt big numbers for YouTube views, Facebook friends and tweets, but not one mentions costs. But a quick calculation can be revealing. In one case it seems the client was paying roughly £120 per exposure.

Thinking about space and time can help too. Global companies are fond of quoting numbers that sound huge. Until you put them in geographical context. Coke's millions of Facebook fans represent fewer than 1% of their user base. Similarly, the fact that the Cadbury 'Gorilla' ad was viewed more than 6 million times online over five years sounds less impressive when you realise that the first TV exposure achieved more than that in a few seconds.

Results should always be compared against objectives. But this is another piece of context that's usually missing. IPA research suggests that few campaigns set clear behavioural objectives at all, let alone specify numerical targets. Historical context is fast becoming impossible to look at. Ironically, in the pre-digital days of sales data coming in on vast scrolls of paper print-outs, we seemed to be more capable of (and interested in) putting sales into historical context. Now it's three years' sales data if you're lucky. And with rapid personnel changes on marketing and agency sides, no-one can learn from the past.

Economists like to put numbers in context by thinking about 'opportunity cost'. What would the numbers have looked like if you'd spent the same money in a different way? This question forces you to find a common currency for evaluation, which can be useful, but rarely happens. So, online reach is measured in terms of views, offline in terms of GRPs (Gross Rating Points) etc. This makes the numbers for online look much bigger, and makes comparisons difficult.

Finally, when presented with that Big Number, try to find out how much variation it conceals. How accurate is it? Could it be a statistical blip? Confidence intervals and statistical significance tests are often brushed over or absent. And there's a more subtle point: many of the numbers that matter in marketing are distributed unevenly. In every category, there tends to be a small core of very heavy users and a much bigger 'long tail' of light users. Averages can be very misleading in these circumstances. Better to go beyond the headline figure and look at how numbers are distributed across the population.

So, next time someone tries to wow you with a Big Number, don't be too easily impressed.

Emotionally, we're all programmed to find big numbers impressive and intimidating. But most numbers are meaningless until placed in context. When someone quotes a large number on its own, they're probably bullshitting.

HOW NOT TO BE SEDUCED BY BIG NUMBERS

2 minute checklist

o   Don't be too impressed by big numbers. In marketing, a million is usually a *small* number.

o   When someone tries to impress you with a big number, put it into context. How big is the market?

o   Prefer percentages to absolute numbers. What percentage of the target market did you reach? And how many times?

o   Get comparable numbers for other kinds of activity. Compare exposures, reach, frequency and GRPs across different media. Creating a 'common currency' may surprise you (see the Wall's ice cream case study earlier in this chapter).

o   Think about costs too. Huge levels of exposure may not be worth it if they cost too much.

o   Compare cost per exposure across different channels. Again, this can be an eye-opener. Cost per exposure can vary by a factor of over 100. Even within the same campaign.

o   Think about conversion rates. Big exposure numbers are less impressive if only 0.1% convert to sales.

Notes:

_____

_____

_____

_____

_____

_____

_____

_____

PUTTING BIG NUMBERS IN CONTEXT
SOCIAL MEDIA

Useful case study

Digital marketers are particularly prone to swinging Big Numbers around. None more so than social media types. Let's put some of the statistics in perspective.

Take Coca-Cola. Back in 2011, Coke became the single most popular brand on Facebook, with over 34 million fans. That's a huge number. Bigger than the population of Canada. At first sight, you might think this a staggeringly successful example of a brand building relationships with its customers online.

But think about the size of Coke. It has around 4 billion users. So those Facebook fans represent a tiny fraction of the user base: less than 1%.

The stats are similarly low for other 'Big' brands on Facebook. The interesting thing is not how many fans these brands have. It's how *few*. Only a minuscule percentage of users seem interested in befriending their brands online.

And it's striking that, even among these hard-core 'fans', talk about the brand is rare. On average, less than 1% of Facebook fans ever bothers to post anything. So active 'fans' probably represent less than one in 10,000 users for most of these brands.

Still impressed by those big social media stats?

Top 10 Facebook brands	Total Facebook Fans	Fans Talking about brand	% fans talking about brand
Coca-Cola	34,511,504	220,867	0.6%
Starbucks	25,446,846	508,526	2.0%
Oreo	23,092,391	114,454	0.5%
Red Bull	22,427,254	112,051	0.5%
Converse All Star	20,141,021	40,858	0.2%
Skittles	19,348,317	137,558	0.7%
PlayStation	17,420,065	104,837	0.6%
Converse	17,420,065	52,866	0.3%
Victoria's Secret	15,343,727	145,125	0.9%
Pringles	13,602,128	50,488	0.4%

Source: Mashable.com, October 2011

HOW ~~NOT~~ TO USE CORRELATIONS

'Male organ and economic growth: does size matter?'
Tatu Westling

A recent *Forbes* article on social media had the headline: 'How valuable are heavy social media users anyway?' It reported that heavy social media users are less likely to buy online than other social media users. When they do, they spend less money too.

Like us, you may have thought this didn't intuitively feel right. Let's look at the analysis in more detail. Plotting heavy, medium and light social media users' buying data, researchers showed that higher social media usage correlated with less online buying and lower spends. From this they deduced that 'heavy social use doesn't translate to desired behaviours'.

This may or may not be true. But it's a nice example of a common research problem: the myth that a correlation 'proves' something to be true. This can lead to muddled and dangerous thinking.

We've noticed how quantitative research companies raise statistical significance issues less often nowadays. Charts used to be peppered with asterisks warning 'small sample size'. But in debriefs now, you often have to ask for sample size and significance. And presenters seem surprised and a bit irritated to be asked. Planners aren't routinely trained to know this stuff these days either.

Forbes doesn't mention statistical significance, but a quick analysis suggests the correlations are almost certainly significant at the 95% confidence level researchers typically use. That raises another issue. Is this 95% level right?

When something is 'significant at 95% confidence' we mean there's only a 5% chance that this result is a statistical fluke.

Once, this was possibly appropriate. But now researchers have more data and more computing power to analyse it. 'Data mining' can churn out hundreds of instant correlations. Meaning fluke results become more common.

This issue is particularly important when research is fuelled by PR agendas. Ever wondered why newspapers are full of articles 'proving' health benefits of various 'superfoods'? Run enough correlations, and you'll always find one making your product look good. Some will even appear statistically significant. But the results are usually a fluke, and rarely replicated.

Natural sciences researchers are familiar with this problem. They raise the standard of proof when running large numbers of correlations. Particle physicists (data miners par excellence) don't treat results as statistically significant unless there's under a one in 2 million chance that it's a fluke (the '5 Sigma' standard). Maybe a bit extreme. But we do need to raise *our* game a bit. And, as all planners should know, correlation doesn't equal causation. And causation is not always what you think it is.

Sometimes the arrow of causality goes the opposite way to expectation. Research routinely shows that people who're aware of communication from brand X are more likely to buy that brand. Sometimes used as evidence that communication drives sales, in fact causality usually runs the other way: buying brand X makes you more likely to notice its communications. This phenomenon (the so-called 'Rosser Reeves effect' – named after the famous 1950s adman) has been known for decades, yet is still routinely used to 'prove' communication effectiveness (most recently to justify social media use).

And sometimes both factors correlate with a third, hidden factor – the real explanation for what's happening. This may be a problem with the *Forbes* research. Heavy social media users tend to be younger. They may also have more time on their hands. Such people tend to have less money, and this may explain why they spend less.

So next time you see a statistical correlation offered as 'proof', be sceptical. Our favourite example comes from an economics research paper: 'Male organ and economic growth: does size matter?' This 'proved' a country's national income correlates with average penis size…

CORRELATION AND CAUSALITY

2 minute checklist

o   Interpret correlations with care. They're
    useful. But they can be misleading.

o   Don't assume a 'strong' correlation is significant. Or a
    weak one isn't. It all depends on the sample size.

o   Always test correlations for statistical significance. Get an
    expert to help. Or find an app.

o   Run significance tests at the right level of confidence: 95%
    confidence is standard, but you should use higher levels when
    doing more than 20 tests (highly likely in a big tracking study or
    data-mining exercise).

o   Remember: correlation is not causation. A correlates with B doesn't
    mean A *causes* B.

o   Watch out for 'reverse causality'. Buying a brand means you're more
    likely to notice its advertising (the 'Rosser Reeves effect'). So sales can
    'cause' ad awareness.

o   Look out for missing variables that affect the ones you're interested
    in. Heavy TV viewers are more likely to buy tabloid newspapers
    because TV viewing and newspaper readership are *both*
    affected by class, income etc.

o   Look for time lags. They can be a useful
    indication of causality. If changes in B *follow*
    changes in A, then B can't cause A. (It doesn't prove
    A causes B though!)

o   Where possible, look for correlations with external factors
    that you can control. Sales can 'cause' ad awareness, but can't
    cause GRPs.

o   Run experiments if you can. Change A and see what happens to
    B. It's the only reliable way to establish causality.

Notes:

_____

_____

_____

_____

_____

_____

_____

_____

TALKING AND THINKING ABOUT STRATEGY

'In all affairs it's a healthy thing now and again to hang a question mark on the things you have long taken for granted'

Bertrand Russell

FIVE

INTRODUCTION

When we consider strategy, we usually focus on where we end up, not on the process of getting there. But there are many factors that influence strategic success. Things we may not give much thought to. Or things we dismiss consciously or unconsciously. This chapter looks at some of these.

So in the first three articles, we consider the strategic thinking mindset. Open-mindedness is important. Too often we planners jump to solutions without doing the necessary research. But successful strategies need us to be open to evidence that challenges our experience, our views or our first strategic hunches. And open to potentially useful learning from other brands, categories or campaigns. Not dismissing these because 'my brand's different' or 'it's all different these days'.

Learning from other people and harnessing the power of brains around us is always a good idea. But group thinking is not without problems. The next two articles examine the pitfalls of collective thinking in general, and the limitations of brainstorming in particular.

Then the last four articles look at the words we choose and use. Words matter a lot in planning. Words shape and limit our strategic thinking. Words are the tools we use to bring our ideas to life. Great strategies are useless if we can't express and sell them to creatives and clients with pithy, evocative words that crackle with energy. In our experience, the best planners always choose 'the best words in the best order'.

HOW ~~NOT~~ TO USE EVIDENCE

'It is a capital mistake to theorise before one has data. Insensibly one begins to twist facts to suit theories, instead of theories to suit facts'
Sherlock Holmes (Arthur Conan Doyle)

When we started writing our 'mythbuster' columns, our main concern was whether we'd run out of myths to bust. We needn't have worried. The world of marketing is full of muddled thinking and dodgy assumptions. But we've often wondered why. Why, when so much time and money is spent on research, and we have more data available than ever, do people so often go with invalid hunches, not the contradictory evidence?

This problem isn't unique to advertising of course. It's such a universal phenomenon that psychologists have a name for it: 'confirmation bias'. This has roots in a cluster of psychological biases, all of which blind us to 'inconvenient truths' that threaten our pet theories.

Our brains look for evidence to confirm our beliefs. We see this every day. Planners rarely come to us looking for help to test their theories. They want evidence to *support* them. And if there's no obvious evidence, they rarely change their point of view. They just ask us to dig deeper.

This desire for confirmation leads us to read articles and blogs that support our point of view and screen out contradictory stuff. And we feel most comfortable when surrounded by like-minded people. In our connected world, it's increasingly possible for us to live in a bubble, isolated from different views. Other professions are no better – even scientists and medics, who really ought to be. And research suggests that training people in proper hypothesis testing really doesn't help much. It seems that this sort of bias is just hardwired in our brains.

The second problem is that, even when evidence contradicts our beliefs, we tend to ignore it. Psychological experiments show that we demand higher standards of proof for things we prefer not to believe. Whereas corroborative evidence tends to go through on the nod. Brain scanning shows that the cognitive dissonance we feel when faced with contradictions makes us work hard to make them go away.

Our tendency to seek confirmation and ignore or deny contradictions is a dangerous combination. It makes us blind to flaws in our theories (Daniel Kahneman calls it 'theory-induced blindness'), and makes us see positive evidence where there isn't any.

Why do our brains work this way? Partly, it's a failure of our reasoning ability. Rigorous hypothesis testing is hard work. Even for data specialists. The ordinary heuristic thinking that all of us (even econometricians) use every day just isn't up to the job. Partly, too, it's because we hate to see our theories

disproved and we indulge in wishful thinking.

Memory also plays a role. Research shows that people remember fake information supporting their beliefs long after being shown that the information is false. In fact, it's not uncommon for contradictory evidence to be remembered as supporting evidence. As a result, attempts to debunk myths often just entrench those myths further.

Finally, social factors are at play. If people find evidence contradicting their theories, they rarely broadcast it. In a world where people surround themselves with like-minded people, this would put them in conflict with everyone around them. Better to sweep evidence under the carpet.

So can anything be done about this tendency to ignore dissonant data? Well, you could employ some people who're experts in hypothesis testing. Or employ heretics who'll challenge the orthodox view. But then, maybe we would say that…

CRITICAL THINKING

2 minute checklist

o   Don't jump to conclusions. You're
    bound to have hunches. And if you're good,
    they may even be right. But keep an open mind.

o   Break out of your bubble. Expose yourself to people who
    don't share your values. Read widely. Get out of the agency.
    Never assume other people think like you.

o   Hire people from different social backgrounds. And with different
    thinking styles.

o   Be sceptical. Question assumptions. Ask the 'obvious', innocent, 'silly'
    or awkward question. Challenge the consensus.

o   Think like a historian. Don't trust conventional narratives, folk tales or
    collective memories. Bear in mind that every storyteller has an agenda.
    Go back to primary data.

o   Think like a scientist. Frame hypotheses. Then look for research and evidence
    to *test* them. If necessary, commission original research or experiment 'in the
    wild' to get the data you need.

o   Check you're still open to alternatives. Are you looking for data to *test* your
    hunch? Or just looking for 'spray-on facts' to 'prove' it?

o   Learn about cognitive biases. Recognise them in yourself.

o   Remember: even 'hard' quantitative data can fool us. We all see patterns
    where there are none. Get a data expert to test your theories.

o   Become a 'learning organisation': share what you learn; learn from
    others; create a central depository of useful knowledge.

HOW TO BECOME A LEARNING ORGANISATION
HEALTHCARE BRAND

Useful case study

Some years ago, a client in the healthcare sector approached us for help with some market research. They wanted to know more about how advertising affected their brand, and they'd identified six key research questions they wanted to answer over the next 12 months. Could we help them come up with a suitable research methodology?

We immediately realised we could do better than that. We'd been working on this brand for many years by then, and had conducted lots of research on it. That meant we already had the answers to their six questions waiting in our files.

We expected the research team to be delighted. But instead they looked crestfallen. They explained that, in a bid to turn their firm into a 'learning organisation', they'd been ordered to research six questions like this every year. If those six questions had already been answered, then they needed to find six new ones, to meet their target.

It seems this had been going on for years. The system meant that the firm spent lots of money on research, but had no incentive to store or learn from the results.

What they really needed was a filing system.

YOUR BRAND IS ~~NOT~~ LIKE OTHER BRANDS

'We all want to be different, which makes us all the same'
Internet meme

Many years ago, we were working on a banking brand. Our main client contact there was a smart data analyst who prided himself on his intimate knowledge of the brand and its millions of users. The brand had started to show signs of stalling. We were trying to find out why.

We started looking at a number of brand measures. Then we asked him what was happening to market share over time. 'Oh, we don't track that. This is finance – it isn't baked beans you know,' was his reply. But when we worked out Share of Market (SOM) and compared it with Share of Voice (SOV) over time, we immediately saw what was causing the brand's problems. In fact, the pattern this simple analysis

revealed was just the same as in other, completely unrelated markets.

The analyst's reply reflects something we come across often: the 'mine's different' syndrome. The symptoms manifest themselves in different forms. Here are some recent examples. 'My market's different' (someone claiming that pain relief brand choice was rationally not emotionally based). 'My country's different' (a client wanting a different ending on a global campaign). 'My users' generation is different' (someone suggesting that people over 50 – ie 'old' to most agency workers – view a category fundamentally differently). Then there's 'My culture's different'. 'My region's different'. 'My brand is different'. 'This decade is different' and so on.

When something is this pervasive, it's helpful to explore why. There seem to us a number of reasons.

Partly, it reflects a human truth: none of us like to be bound by rules. And this may be an even stronger impulse in fields like ours, where creativity is important. As familiar as we all are with evidence of our herd-like and copying instincts, we also want to feel different, special and individual. To discover that our pet food brand is pretty similar to other pet food brands, or the ethically conscious buyers of our new food brand behave similarly to the global brand leader, can be hard to accept. It also reflects how many people are just unaware there are cross-market rules at all. As an industry we're great at junking historic data and re-inventing the wheel.

Why does this 'mine's different' syndrome matter though?

It's certainly responsible for lots of the politics and subjective debate that blight meetings and slow timing plans. But most importantly, it matters because if we always act on the assumption that 'mine's different' we can't learn from what's happened before. And so we carry on repeating the same mistakes.

There's an important caveat here. Patterns can only explain so much. Marketing and communication by numbers would be a disaster.

At heart, creativity is about breaking rules, not sticking to them. There are similarities between humans across all cultures, but also important differences. Global communication needs to be attuned to this, so we tread the fine line between cultural faux pas and bland lowest common denominator. The skill for us in marketing communication is balance. We need to manage this tension between difference and similarity, pattern and distinctiveness. We always liked the way this was summed up by a teenage girl in a research group who said, 'I want to be different – just like my friends.'

LEARNING FROM OTHER BRANDS

2 minute checklist

o   Never assume your problem
    is unique. Others will have faced this
    before. Learn from them.

o   Know the general 'rules' for effective marketing.
    Understand how these rules vary by context. Use data and
    evidence to understand precisely when the rules can be flexed.

o   Use some simple analysis 'basics' when you start work on new
    brands. Compare SOV against SOM. And penetration against
    frequency. Understand how these metrics behave in your category.

o   Learn from other categories. Selling insurance is not the same as
    selling soap powder. But there are similarities. Study brands from other
    sectors that have tackled problems like yours.

o   Learn from other countries. Cultural differences are important. But the
    fundamentals of psychology, economics and marketing are similar everywhere.
    Anyone tried this strategy elsewhere? Any brands in other markets you can
    learn from?

o   Resist the urge to reject ideas 'not invented here'. Your brand isn't as
    special as you think.

o   Don't assume your brand is different. It probably behaves much like
    other brands in its category. Breaking category rules is hard – and
    usually requires a radically different product or service.

o Don't assume your buyers are
   different. Your customers will be similar
   to competitors'. They may well be the same people.
o Resist the urge to create differences where there aren't
   any. Be sceptical about segmentation studies dividing people
   into neat, snappily named groups.
o Be cynical about any label beginning 'Generation'. Ditto 'Millennials'
   (more on Millennials later in this chapter). Generational differences
   are smaller than you think.
o Learn from the past. New technology and social trends bring new problems
   and tools to solve them. But the fundamentals of marketing
   are surprisingly stable.
o Familiarise yourself with your brand's history. Read old IPA and APG papers
   on the brand and competitors.
o Look outside marketing completely. Note how Great Ormond Street
   Hospital partnered with Formula 1 pit-stop crews to learn how to improve
   the speed and efficiency of patient handover from operating theatre to
   intensive care unit.

THE PAST IS ~~NOT~~ RELEVANT

'Many people get obsessed by what's in the foreground, when the
background may have a greater part to play'
Terence Conran

You don't need to read industry surveys to know that most people who work in advertising and marketing are pretty young. That means two things: lots of us don't know much about anything that happened beyond the immediate past; and those of us that do, don't like to mention it in case we look old.

This lack of historical perspective is compounded by the fact that advertising people tend, by nature, to be forward-looking creatures interested in shiny new things. And ad agencies are constantly looking for new ways to differentiate themselves.

The net result: an obsession with what's new and what's changing. It's almost obligatory now for any presentation to kick off with the

mantra, 'Everything's changing, and it's never changed so fast as now'. Ironic, though, that this obsession with the new is actually very old. As management guru Tom Peters said: 'It is the arrogance of modernity to believe we face unprecedented changes – what people say now about the internet, they used to say about radio, the telegraph and the railways.'

If we *are* all too obsessed with novelty and change, does it matter? Yes, for several reasons.

First, it stops us from learning from the past. A few years back, an academic programme reviewed what as an industry we know about how marketing communications work. If we exclude the work of the Ehrenberg-Bass Institute, it was striking how little we've learned in the last 100 years.

Our lack of historical perspective limits our learning. Old data is routinely binned (anyone seen a 5-year sales trend recently?). Old case studies are forgotten. And even when we do know the past, we reject its lessons because 'it's all different this time'. In finance (an industry said to be dominated by people who know too much maths and not enough history), this logic led to the 'Dotcom Bubble', the Enron collapse and the 'Credit Crunch'. It's equally disastrous in our world.

Secondly, our obsession with what's changing distracts us from what *hasn't* changed. We tend to assume any new technology will sweep away the old stuff. PVRs (Personal Video Recorders) are killing live TV. The internet is killing both of them. And social media is killing advertising. In fact, new technology tends to co-exist with old technologies for surprisingly long periods of time. As anyone who's studied the effect of TV on radio, or radio on print, understands.

Most importantly, the obsession with the new distracts us from what *doesn't* change: human nature. As always, Bill

Bernbach understood this years ago: 'Human nature hasn't changed for a million years. It won't even change in the next million years. Only the superficial things have changed. It is fashionable to talk about the changing man. A communicator must be concerned with the unchanging man – what compulsions drive him, what instincts dominate his every action, even though his language too often camouflages what really motivates him.'

Bernbach anticipated the latest thinking about our brain. Our conscious 'System 2' thoughts are changeable. But behaviour is mostly driven by the unconscious, automatic processing of 'System 1' – older, and not nearly so changeable. Most of our mental apparatus is unchanged since we discovered fire.

So don't get too distracted by the shiny new and changing stuff. When it comes to how marketing works, what historian David Edgerton called 'the shock of the old' is more helpful than the allure of the new.

THINKING ABOUT CHANGE

2 minute checklist

o   Always look at the historic data on your
    brand and category. Two or three years' data isn't
    enough – look at long-term trends.
o   Use syndicated sources like Mintel and TGI to get a wider
    view. 'Old school' maybe, but still indispensable. Use
    government (ONS) data and specialist consultancies to get
    really long-term trends.
o   Look for trend data online: Google Trends for search behaviour,
    Google Ngram Viewer for cultural trends over centuries.
o   Remember: understanding politics, history and cultural evolution is
    part of our job. Know what happened during the last economic crisis,
    and you're better prepared for the next one.
o   Hire people with a long-term perspective. They might be history graduates.
    Or they might just be older, with more experience.
o   Create a brand archive. Gather useful data and research. Document
    successes and failures. Make sure it's updated, maintained and used.

o   Don't get obsessed with what's changing.
    Ask what's *unchanging* about your brand, buyers
    and category. The things that *don't* change are often
    the most surprising.
o   Don't write off marketing and research techniques just
    because they're old. The oldest ones can sometimes be the most
    effective.
o   Be wary when someone says, 'It's different this time'. It's often a
    prelude to disaster.

LEARNING FROM THE PAST
FOOD BRAND

Useful case study

A couple of years ago, the owners of a food brand asked us to help with the launch of a new variant. Sales of the core product had been stagnant for a while. But they were going to change all that with a programme of new product launches. Preliminary research had identified the first potential winner: a new flavour and format which would expand the brand into a different sector, potentially expanding the range of usage occasions. Now all we needed to do was to think about how to launch it.

We listened politely to their ambitious sales targets, then asked if they realised this product had been launched before.

The clients were astounded to discover that their predecessors had tried to launch exactly the same new product in the UK 15 years before, with similarly ambitious targets. Unfortunately, it was a flop, and was withdrawn a year or so later. Further research showed the same idea had been tried in other markets around the world, with similarly disappointing results.

Shortly after that, the marketing team turned its attention back to the core product. And the story has a happy ending. The team invested in a great new ad campaign for the core product, and sales started growing again. But things might not have worked out so well without that little history lesson.

145

Notes:

_____

_____

_____

_____

_____

_____

_____

HOW ~~NOT~~ TO HARNESS OUR COLLECTIVE BRAINPOWER

'Boaty McBoatface wins poll to name polar research vessel'
The Guardian, April 2016

At a recent brainstorming session, discussion turned to promoting a new product. Someone casually mentioned an upcoming big public event. Could we organise some kind of stunt there? The group seized on this thought and quickly came up with half a dozen ideas. It looked like we'd cracked it.

But then someone pointed out that there was little overlap between our target audience and the crowd at the event. The timing was wrong too. Suddenly the idea looked stupid. How could we have been so dumb?

Military strategists would recognise this problem: groups make reckless decisions by latching on to any proposal for action, rather than thinking more deeply.

But for 20 years it's become more fashionable to focus on the strengths of collective thinking rather than any weaknesses. The big influence, clearly, is the internet, where the success of open-source projects like Linux and Wikipedia convince us that crowdsourcing is the future. Economists praise the efficiency of markets and the 'wisdom of crowds'. Co-creation is the order of the day. The ad industry has embraced this enthusiastically. Brainstorming was invented by an adman (more about him in the next article); 70 years later, we're still doing it, still spending lots of time 'sharing', 'huddling' and 'looping in'.

Technology plays a role too. Electronic calendars mean more meetings are crammed into each day. Teleconferencing means distance is no object. Smartphones mean everyone is contactable. And agencies have accelerated this trend, removing barriers to shared working. Open-plan offices are de rigeur, and ideas are crowdsourced online. In this brave new world, all work is group work. All problems solved by the 'hive mind'.

But while some collaboration is fruitful, some isn't. Research repeatedly concludes that brainstorming is bad at generating ideas. Open-plan offices reduce productivity, especially for creative and analytical work. In fact, most people say they do their best thinking when alone and relaxed (often in the bath or shower). As a result, increasing numbers of us have to escape the office these days to get the real work done.

If collective thinking is unproductive, collective decision making can be downright dangerous. Groups try to avoid conflict, so tend to suppress dissent and reject 'inconvenient truths'. Social psychologists call this 'groupthink', blaming it for disastrous mistakes such as the Iraq invasion and sub-prime crisis. Investment bubbles remind economists that 'herd behaviour' causes crowds to make poor decisions. In all these crises,

the lone wolves made the right call. And the group thinkers got it wrong.

So how can we get the best from our collective intelligence? 'Prediction markets' give us a clue. Research shows that crowds only make accurate judgments when everyone thinks independently. As soon as people start thinking together, judgement gets clouded. This is the key to the success of open source. Linux and Wikipedia were built by people who mostly thought and worked in isolation, then got together afterwards to share and critique each other's ideas.

Creativity, intelligence and innovation are the lifeblood of our business. They all require independent thought. So forget about brainstorming, huddles and endless meetings. We need time and space to think alone. Technology companies are aware of this. Google's London office has a proper old-fashioned library for people to work in, with a strict policy of silence. Maybe it's time to celebrate the power of disconnection.

HOW ~~NOT~~ TO BRAINSTORM

'Once the miracle of creation has taken place, the group can build and
extend it, but the group never invents anything'
John Steinbeck

You may not have heard of Alex Osborn, one of the 1950s 'Mad Men'. But you'll almost certainly have taken part in something he bequeathed to our world. Because it's Mr Osborn who's credited with originating the business use of the term and technique of 'brainstorming'.

Frustrated by how, in his opinion, group decision-making processes tended to inhibit not encourage creative thinking, his new technique supposedly increased the quality and quantity of ideas generated. With 'rules' of no censoring of ideas, quantity over quality and an informal atmosphere, the brainstorm was supposed to unleash the creative in all of us. Many Post-it notes and hours

in hotel conference rooms later, the technique lives on nowadays in one guise or another.

But does brainstorming actually work? We've spent hundreds of hours in these sessions over the years. But we can't recall a single great idea that came out of all that expensively choreographed management time.

Academic research agrees. Over the years it's been demonstrated unequivocally that brainstorming groups produce fewer and poorer quality ideas than the same number of people working alone. As mentioned in the last article, you're more likely to come up with a great idea in your bath than in a

Holiday Inn meeting room.

Research shows there are many psychological processes at work which together limit the effectiveness of brainstorming. 'Social loafing' — a group situation encourages and allows individuals to slack off. 'Evaluation apprehension' — we're nervous of being judged by colleagues or looking stupid. 'Production blocking' — because only one person can speak at a time in a group, others can forget or reject their ideas while they wait. We're also learning more about the power of our 'herd' tendencies. As humans, we have innate desires to conform to others with only the slightest encouragement. When asked to think creatively, these implicit norms are invisible but powerful shackles on our ability to think differently. No wonder so few ideas emerge.

So why do we keep doing these brainstorms? Even if we're not aware of research on their ineffectiveness, the lack of good ideas coming from them should be obvious to everyone. The answer is probably that holding brainstorms meets other, unarticulated, needs. These compensate for the lack of creativity — time out of the office maybe? A chance for team bonding? And getting a brainstorm in the diary

can make it feel that at least *something's* being done to tackle a tricky issue.

Luckily, there's also useful research showing ways to make brainstorming sessions more productive. Experiments using online brainstorms found that when people typed their ideas at the same time as seeing other people's ideas displayed, more and better ideas were generated. This neatly got around those psychological processes blocking the effectiveness of face-to-face sessions.

So here's how to get the best of both worlds. If you want a face-to-face brainstorm to work, ask people to list ideas on their own, in the bath or wherever, before coming to the session. Monitor the number of ideas produced by each person. Then use the group to evaluate ideas generated. Because psychological research shows that while groups aren't great at coming up with ideas, they're very good at evaluating them.

A brainstorm is defined as 'a sudden disturbance of the mind'. If you want your experience of them to be a bit more positive than this, you've hopefully now got some evidence to help.

COLLECTIVE THINKING

2 minute checklist

o   Harness collective thinking carefully. Get it wrong, and it can be inefficient, unproductive or downright dangerous.

o   Hire and use diverse thinkers. Look for people who think critically and ask awkward questions. Not people who 'fit in'.

o   Don't underestimate the power of solo thinking. Many of the best thinkers are introverts. And most people do their best thinking when they're alone.

o   Create and protect space in your diary to think, read, analyse or muse. Don't let the day fill up with pointless meetings.

o   Get out of the office and sit in a park or café. Let your mind wander. Ideas pop up when 'we're looking the other way'. Not sitting at our desks.

o   Don't let email distract you. Copy Googlers: only dip into email twice a day. Think twice before you send emails; they just beget more emails. Don't copy in people unnecessarily.

o   Don't default to a brainstorming session. Find smarter, more efficient ways to harness collective brainpower.

o   Separate the generation and evaluation of
    ideas. Brief people on the problem before sessions,
    to think individually or in pairs. Give them time to mull
    it over.

o   Use group sessions for sharing, evaluating and developing
    ideas, not generating them.

o   Use online forums to allow people to share some of this strategic
    spadework.

o   Tread carefully when harnessing the 'wisdom of crowds'– remember
    Boaty McBoatface.

o   Use more sophisticated voting techniques, such as prediction markets,
    if you want to tap public opinion.

HOW ~~NOT~~ TO CHOOSE WORDS

'I know words. I have the best words'
Donald J Trump

In his essay 'Politics and the English language', George Orwell complained how bad language, his 'worn out and useless words', meant muddled thinking. We agree. A lot of marketing-speak is bollocks.

First, we use words that don't inspire. We spray ugly 'worn out' words like 'engagement' over strategy documents and briefs. We default to tired, banal adjectives when describing brand personalities: 'warm', 'accessible', 'confident' and so on. We use language we'd never use in daily conversations. Cue the company priding itself on its marketing skills, describing their target as 'active boomers – joy-embracers who've experienced what's important to them and learned to treasure meaningful pleasure moments'. Not easy for any creative team to feel inspired by those words.

This marketing-speak is frighteningly common. To be fair, it can be hard to avoid when faced with the need for international 'alignment'. But we work in creative industries. Let's choose simple, fresh and evocative words which inspire and enlighten.

Next, we have the words which dehumanise and distance us from the task at the heart of our jobs: understanding real people. Don't use inhuman words such as 'consumer', 'housewife' or 'Millennial'. Try inserting the word 'people' instead of 'consumers'. You immediately sense how this distancing effect works.

Maybe because of its historic focus on the technological vs the human, digital marketing seems particularly prone to dehumanising language. In *Campaign* recently, a 'digital expert' claimed that 'consumers are expecting to participate as co-creators in their chosen media space, and are looking to engage in consumer-generated content'. Apart from being horrible to read, this sort of jargon only increases the distance between ourselves and the people we're trying to understand and talk to.

Finally, there are the words with in-built flawed assumptions. Step forward all those plans aiming to encourage 'active engagement', make ads more 'persuasive', 'force reappraisal', 'strengthen the brand–consumer relationship', 'drive brand loyalty', and so on. These words all sound harmless enough, but the assumptions and principles built into them are flawed. That means they knock marketing effectiveness off course. By and large, people don't want to 'actively engage' or have 'strong relationships' with brands, advertising or even 'consumer-generated content'. And they don't need to for marketing to be successful. Communication can work without 'persuasion' or 'reappraisal'. In fact, it needn't actually 'communicate' much at all. And as we've said before, brand loyalty is largely an irrelevance.

It's probably no coincidence that most of these words portray advertising as a powerful force, causing dramatic shifts in behaviour. People in our industry love macho words like 'driving', 'forcing' and 'active'. They make us feel in control. But they don't reflect reality.

Looking at how real people think, feel and act, we find marketing is usually a weak influence, nudging us just slightly towards one brand or another. This may still be highly profitable. But it's a much less macho affair than most marketing language suggests.

Criticising the words we use may seem pedantic and over-intellectual. In fact, it's the most practical thing imaginable. Sloppy language leads to sloppy thinking, ineffective creative work and wasted money. If we want to serve our clients well, we need to choose our words well.

THE POWER OF A WELL-CHOSEN WORD
2012 OLYMPICS

Useful case study

In a social media-driven and 24-hour news world, how on earth do you give 60,000 people a preview of what millions can't wait to see… yet manage to persuade them to keep schtum about it for five days? The answer: you choose your words smartly. Danny Boyle, London 2012 Olympics Artistic Director, displayed a genius understanding of both human nature and the power of the right word when he asked the lucky attendees of his Opening Ceremony dress rehearsal to '#SaveTheSurprise'. Because amazingly, everyone did. How different would it have been, though, if instead had Danny asked them to 'Keep It Secret'? The words seem so similar. But the canny choice of the word 'surprise' rather than 'secret' made all the difference. Everyone wants to know and tell a secret. We can't help ourselves. It's human nature. But no-one wants to spoil a surprise, or have a surprise spoiled. The persuasive power of the words we choose… Choose them carefully.

Notes:

_____

_____

_____

_____

_____

_____

_____

_____

HOW ~~NOT~~ TO USE THE P-WORD

'The best lack all conviction, while the worst are full of passionate intensity'
WB Yeats

We buy a certain breakfast cereal regularly. It's a great product. It has a history of great advertising. And we much prefer it to its rivals. But one thing about it annoys us. On the side of the pack is a little paragraph headed 'Made with Passion'.

'Passion' is one of the most overused words in the business lexicon. It's not just trite. It's inappropriate. It leads to flawed thinking and strategy. We're so used to hearing people banging on about how passionate they are about something, we seem to have forgotten what the word means.

Excluding religious senses of the word, 'passion' generally refers to strong emotions apt to burst out in violent ways. Passion is usually irrational,

transient and uncontrollable. It's an unhinged state of mind. That's why the French legal system used to recognise the *crime passionnel* as a valid defence in some murder cases. Tellingly, American courts refer to this as 'temporary insanity'.

Of course, when cereal brands or C-suite types say they're 'passionate' about their business, most don't intend to give that impression. They mean something different.

When the makers of our cereal brand explain their 'passion and dedication', they refer to the quality of their ingredients and the care with which they process them. And we believe them. Our experience of the product, and what we know about how it's produced, suggests that this is a company that does go to great pains to produce excellent stuff. But that's not the result of an outburst of passion. It's the result of employing trained staff, following well thought-out production processes, and enforcing rigorous quality standards. These things – rational, long term and highly controlled – are the opposite of 'passion'.

'So what?' you might say, 'it's just a bit of overused but harmless business-speak'.

We don't think so. Last week we bought a take-away from a fast-food outlet. As the surly kid behind the counter handed over the dodgy food, we noticed a sign behind him saying 'Passionate about Quality and Service'. When the gap between the corporate rhetoric of passion and the everyday reality experienced by customers gets that big, brands become a laughing stock.

Turning to the people who buy brands, they're rarely passionate about any of them. Despite what marketing people hope or like to think. Indifference is a more helpful and realistic frame of mind to work with to achieve successful strategies.

Occasionally we encounter a genuine display of passion in the business world (a couple of our clients had a fist-fight recently!). But it's rare. And nearly always a bad thing. Good leaders are usually the opposite of passionate: they're calm, controlled and stick to their vision without being blown off course by emotional outbursts.

There are of course examples of passionate leadership – although they're more common in religion and politics than business. Charismatic preachers really do use passion to sway huge congregations. Populists like Donald Trump simulate passion when they want to stir the mob. But this is the stuff of mass hysteria. Not long-term business success. And it's striking how often these people turn out to be frauds. Once you start faking passion to get things done, other deceptions follow quite easily.

So there you have it. In the world of marketing, anyone who says they're passionate is misguided, a liar or a lunatic. 'The worst are full of passionate intensity'.

YOU DO ~~NOT~~ NEED TO SPELL IT OUT

'It seems to me you should use their language, the language they use every day, the language in which they think'
David Ogilvy

Last week, we were sent a presentation updating us on a brand's sales performance. We started going through the charts. But by page 4 we gave up. The graphs were easy to understand; the titles, though, were not. By chart 4, helpfully titled 'P4W Drinkers ROI other LAD', we were thinking WTF?

So this article is devoted to EUA (Excessive Use of Acronyms). Using acronyms in business is nothing new. But it does feel like it's getting out of hand. A simple query around the office unleashed a torrent of examples and pleas for EUA to be wrestled under control. We came across SLF ('Self Loading Freight' – what one train operator calls its passengers); BM (used intriguingly by the same company for both Brand Manager and Bowel Movement); and even one client who'd issued a helpful glossary of company acronyms to its agencies. This ran to 13 pages and over 200 examples (FFS!).

Why is this happening? We suspect it's partly to do with standardisation. As companies grow bigger and more global, and business methods become professionalised, business people around the world are increasingly using the same practices. The same terminology becomes used more frequently and across the organisation – fertile breeding ground for common acronyms. Technology has probably played a role too. Anyone who's tried expressing themselves within the confines of a PowerPoint headline, text (OMG) or tweet will know how seductive acronyms can be.

What's wrong with convenient shorthand you might ask? We're all busy – it's impractical to say and write longhand versions of all the words we regularly use in business life. Acronyms oil the wheels. Speed things up. It could even be argued that a shared vocabulary of acronyms unintelligible to people outside an organisation can be a force for good, creating a sense of community and shared culture.

All this may be true. But there are dangers when it goes too far. Acronyms that help speed up communication internally are often unintelligible when they move into the real world. Worse, they can be a great smokescreen for the lazy or less competent to hide behind. Sprinkling your PowerPoint presentation with acronyms is a great way to make your work look complex and scientific. Even when it's vacuous. And if other people can't understand what you're writing or saying, maybe you feel a bit cleverer too.

Acronyms also have a dangerous distancing effect. We've said this before regarding 'consumer' – use it and you immediately lose all sense of real people.

But perhaps our biggest concern about EUA is that there's a fine line between making something shorter so it's quicker to say and write, and making it shorter so it needs less thought. When acronyms take on a life of their own, people often stop thinking about the assumptions that lie behind them.

Some think that the innocent-looking acronym may even have played a part in the sub-prime crisis America experienced some years back. Maybe it's no coincidence that some of its culprits were distinguished by TLAs (Three Letter Acronyms). Think about CDOs (Collateralised Debt Obligations) and CDSs (Credit Default Swaps). Just writing them longhand, with the words 'debt' and 'default' exposed, somehow makes them look less innocent.

So, keep using your acronyms. But make sure your use is BIC (Best in Class) and WBN (Well Below Normal). Otherwise, STFU.

WORDS WE CANNOT DO WITHOUT

'The limits of my language mean the limits of my world'
Ludwig Wittgenstein

At the end of any year, it's customary to compile a list: predictions for the New Year. Or highlights of the year gone by. At the end of 2015, we offered another list: words we'd like to see the back of. Some because they were plain irritating. Others because they were misleading or damaging.

Words and thinking are intertwined. Sloppy thinking leads to sloppy language. More significantly, nonsense words can distort the way we think. So here is our 2015 Dishonours word list.

Engagement: a vague, catch-all term covering any kind of consumer response. Engagement is always crucial for 'driving consumers' and delivering a high 'ROI'. People talking 'engagement' usually live in an alternative universe where 'consumers' care 'passionately' about brands. This is odd, because 'engagement metrics' usually tell us that nobody gives a monkey's.

Reaching out: a US export, this started life as a polite introductory phrase between people collaborating across the Atlantic. Now every email, phone call or conversation seems to involve 'reaching out' to someone. Whatever happened to just 'writing' or 'talking'?

Big Data: this one actually means something, even if it is rather vague: 'Big Data' is too large to be handled using standard data-processing applications. If you're analysing data from the Large Hadron Collider, that's 'Big Data'. If you're analysing a customer database, that's just 'data'. Ad agencies usually work with 'small data', and get rather confused by it.

Connecting: another Americanism used to describe people talking to one another. See 'Engagement' and 'Reaching out'.

Message: traditionally the raison d'être of advertising, especially for the client. Largely ignored by ordinary people, and often unrelated to sales. Now increasingly superseded by 'content'.

Sharing: the most valuable kind of 'connecting'. Only achieved when there are high levels of 'engagement'. When 'consumers' share your content, 'ROI' is maximised. This almost never happens.

Deep diving: a phrase designed to make us all feel cleverer than we really are. Who doesn't feel like they're really getting into the nitty-gritty of something with a 'deep dive' instead of a 'review' or even an 'analysis'? For maximum effect, combine with 'Big Data'.

Content: nobody knows what this means, so it can mean anything you like.

Driving: almost always the precursor to 'to our website' or some other part of the digital 'ecosystem'. It's an annoying word because it's used so much. But it's also dangerous, because it implies that marketing has a much stronger and more immediate influence than is really the case. See 'Engagement'.

ROI: short for 'Return on Investment', this is a financial term. So, we naturally tend to use it for things unrelated to finance, like 'engagement' metrics. When it is used in a financial sense, most of us get the sums wrong. And even if we get the sums right, ROI is usually the wrong metric on which to focus.

Real-time planning: an oxymoron. Planning is something you do ahead of time. 'Real-time planning' is what normal people call 'reacting'. Usually to short-term 'engagement' metrics, ideally using 'Big Data', in a bid to maximise short-term 'ROI'. None of these things relate well to long term profits. So real-time planning can be a good way to destroy your business.

Aligning: what marketing folks do when they've finished 'reaching out', 'connecting' and 'deep diving'. What normal people call 'agreeing'. Whenever people in marketing and advertising 'align' themselves with something, you can usually bet it's wrong.

LANGUAGE

2 minute checklist

o Be alert to the words you use. They matter
   – a lot.

o Say things simply and clearly. If you can't, your thinking
   is muddled.

o Write like you talk. Or better, like your mum talks. She
   wouldn't talk about 'driving consumers to a content hub'.
   Neither should you.

o Avoid clichés, jargon and dead language. Look for new ways of
   saying things.

o Only use technical language when ordinary words won't do.

o Be careful with words from science, technology or finance. They all
   have precise meanings. Use them correctly, or not at all.

o Look out for hidden assumptions in the words you use. Call it an
   'awareness campaign', and you define the role for advertising.

o Write, take a break, then go back to it. Subtly adjust your words.
   Does that make it better? 'Marmite is *forgotten* at the back of the
   cupboard' is true. 'Marmite is *neglected*' was an award-winning
   creative springboard.

o Avoid bland, tired words. Your brand needs a distinctive
   personality. Your writing should reflect it.

o   Try defining personality as a sentence. Avoid
    banal word lists: 'open', 'honest', 'down to earth yet
    aspirational' and all that nonsense.
o   Use concrete, vivid words. Words evoking visual images
    are particularly powerful.
o   Watch out for words that dehumanise. Never write
    'consumers', 'Millennials' or 'housewives'.
o   Use metaphors. They bring colour and energy. Our brains sing when
    we hear them. 'The George Clooney of toffees' – five words that say
    so much.
o   Learn the rules of rhetoric: the science of how to use words to
    influence people. Aristotle can help you write better brand manifestos.
o   Don't lapse into hyperbole or empty bombast. You're selling biscuits,
    not invading Poland. Avoid self-deceptive, macho language.
o   If you want to change the culture, change the language. Language
    shapes thinking and behaviour.
o   Never assume people from other cultures are taking out the
    meaning you intend. Use visuals, archetypes and metaphors
    to clarify.

Notes:

_____

_____

_____

_____

_____

_____

_____

_____

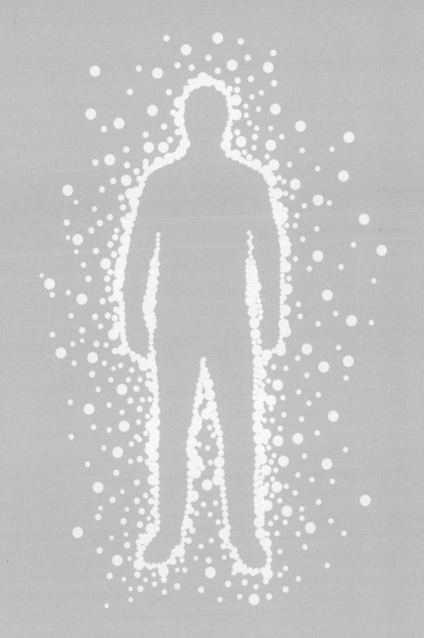

WHO ARE YOU
TALKING TO?

'I don't know how to talk to everybody, only to somebody'

Howard Gossage

food market wasn't segmented

Actually, our client shouldn't ha
surprised. Anyone familiar
late Andrew Ehrenberg's wor
brand segmentation is a r
myth. Ehrenberg analysed man
across many categories and
He analysed user attitudes, lifes
demographics. His conclusior
segmentation hardly exists, if a

Ehrenberg found that, within
category, there are sometime
that are bit different. So, luxur
behave like a separate category
rest of the car market. The b
richer for a start. But when it
competition *within* a sector, El
data showed that a buyer is a
buyer. Difference in user profiles
brands is nearly always minimal.

So brand buyers know and
brand. But they rarely view th
as different from the others in t
And that's why they're never
loyal to any one of these bran
saw with our baby food buye
more than happy to buy ri
from time to time.

Ehrenberg's data suggests

SIX ●

INTRODUCTION

Who are you talking to? Such a simple question.

But get this wrong and your strategy is built on sand. And it's surprising how often we do get it wrong: dodgy segmentations ('Muesli Mums'), fake targets ('Millennials'), and lazy thinking ('it's all different now folks').

The theme running through all this chapter's articles is the danger of targeting based on ungrounded assumptions and received wisdom.

We start with a view on market segmentation – or rather the lack of it. It's widely assumed that targeting means focusing ruthlessly on the precise part of the market your brand appeals to. Thinking up alliterative names for different 'consumer segments' has long amused planners in idle moments. But these segments are not just harmless distractions; they're based on flawed understanding of how brands work. The result is flawed strategy and limited

brand growth.

The truth is, markets are less segmented than we assume. Successful brands have broad appeal. So it's crucial that planners understand the 'typical' person. Unfortunately, advertising people are far from typical. This distorts our perception of the world. Our second article explores these biases and how to overcome them.

Because agency people are young, our intuitions about age are particularly distorted. The third and fourth articles in this chapter explore our obsession with Millennials. And our neglect of other ages where, in the West at least, wealth and brand opportunity reside.

Finally, we look at how an 'in the mirror' approach to planning warps our views on social change and its impact. We get so seduced by what's changing among the few, that we miss what's staying the same among the many. The final three articles offer a more balanced view on social trends.

YOUR BU

'Brands are not the
them as, but sho

We were once aske
qualitative research into
research brief was caref
do groups among mc
aged between six and
we'd split the groups a
brand of baby food they

So we had a group who
a new premium, organi
pouches; another group
established, more seriou
in pots; and a third grou
cheap and cheerful jar bra
was to explore differenc
their attitudes towards th
food is a 'high interest
there was one. The bra
felt very different to us. Sc
behind the one-way mi
the differences between
bought these brands.

SEGMENTATION

2 minute checklist

o   Don't think about targeting and 'owning'
    customer segments. Brands usually grow by
    recruiting buyers from *all* segments.

o   Don't think of them as 'your' consumers. Real people
    regard brands within a category as fairly interchangeable,
    and swap frequently between them.

o   Focus on how *many* people buy your brand, more than who
    those buyers are. Appeal to *all* category buyers.

o   Don't neglect light buyers – they're more important than you think.

o   Don't underestimate how promiscuous your buyers are. Many
    Waitrose shoppers also shop at Lidl. Many *Guardian* readers read the
    Daily Mail from time to time.

o   Never assume another brand isn't a threat because it 'appeals to a
    different segment'. You compete with *every* brand in your category.

o   Note: there are exceptions. Brands that differ in terms of function,
    distribution or price may appeal to different need states (although
    the people buying may be the same).

o If there *are* big differences in usage, divide your market into sectors. Separate sports cars from hatchbacks. Women's shoes from men's.

o But don't be seduced by 'niche marketing'. Most 'niche' brands are really just… small.

o Interpret and use segmentation data with care.

o Pay more attention to absolute numbers than indices. An over-index on under 24s, for example, might be less important than the fact that still 60% of users are over 40.

o Be sceptical about cluster analyses dividing markets into neat, well-defined segments. Especially when the segmentation is attitudinal.

o Use media segmentation data to maximise reach, rather than to target narrow segments.

SEGMENTATION
WHISKY BRAND

Useful case study

Some years ago, a planner came to us for help with a whisky brand she was working on. She wanted to know what made drinkers of this brand different from other whisky drinkers. Was it an age thing? Or was it more of an attitude to life?

We duly trawled through TGI data, looking for significant differences. We looked at income and education, age and gender. We looked at hundreds of lifestyle statements. In fact, we looked at every single criterion on the TGI questionnaire.

And the answer was exactly as expected. Once confidence levels were adjusted to account for the large number of statistical tests involved (a necessity in data-mining exercises of this kind), it became apparent that there were *no* significant differences. None at all.

In fact, there were no significant differences between *any* of the mainstream whisky brands. They all appealed to exactly the same sorts of people. The only brands that had a different customer profile were the single malts. And even then, differences were slight. Single malt drinkers were a bit older and richer. That's all.

So the whisky market could be divided into just two sectors – blends and single malts – and neither sector was segmented. If you're selling blended whisky, your target market is blended whisky drinkers. If you're selling single malt, your target is people who drink single malts. And those two groups of people are actually pretty similar, because they overlap massively.

Who said targeting was complicated?

Notes:

_____

_____

_____

_____

_____

_____

_____

_____

YOU'RE ~~NO~~ DIFFERENT

'Advertising has become marketing by selfie stick'
Bob Hoffman

Two seemingly unrelated things happened to us last year; they made us worried.

First, a young planner was telling us why she likes working on digital stuff more than TV. 'People spend loads more time online than watching TV these days,' she said. We pointed out that data actually shows that people, even young ones, still spend lots more time watching TV. 'Oh, I don't believe that,' she said, 'I mean, I don't…'

Next day we were in a bungalow on a housing estate just outside Manchester. We were talking to a group of women in their 60s about a holiday home brand. We hadn't met them before, but they shared their concerns and hopes in a way that was fascinating, funny and thought-provoking. Perched on stools in that sitting room, we were ashamed to realise we couldn't remember the last time we'd spoken to anyone in face-to-face research outside London.

Is there a link between these two observations? When the world's supposedly more open and connected than ever, are planners (ironically) becoming more insulated and isolated from the 'real world'?

All of us have a tendency to assume we're typical. Psychologists talk about the 'typical mind fallacy' ('other people are just like me'); 'false consensus bias' ('everyone else thinks like me'); and 'confirmation bias' ('yes, I am right'). Our digital, multi-channel world exaggerates these effects. The internet makes it easier than ever to meet like-minded souls, and find sources of information that match our views. It's too easy to construct a media bubble, where everything we see or read confirms our preconceptions. Without contrasting points of view, our thinking becomes more detached from reality.

Planners make similar mistakes. Pushed for time and money, it's ever harder to get out of the agency. Let alone trek up the motorway to do groups outside of London. Far cheaper and quicker to use the internet. Or do a quick survey of agency staff. Or read another planner's blog.

Trapped in our advertising bubble, it's easy to lapse into making stuff for people like ourselves. But our audiences are usually very different: older, poorer, more female, less London-centric, less educated, more likely to have kids or grandchildren. And with very different media habits. One of our great young planners used to remind himself of this with a Post-it note above his desk saying, 'Remember: people who buy new cars are *old*!'

If we're to avoid losing touch with our audiences, we have to connect and talk to them – preferably face to face. We were appalled when a planner recently confessed he'd never talked face to face with any of his target audiences during his career. New digital techniques ('mobile ethnography' etc) are of course useful sometimes. But we've always felt that the value of old-style focus groups lay as much in simply getting out of the agency and into people's houses as what was said in those houses in the 'real' research.

Of course, you don't even have to 'do research' to get out of your bubble. The late great BMP creative John Webster attributed much of his popular success to his deliberate shunning of the 'ad world', and preference instead for discussing his ideas with Pat the office tea lady or Ray the building manager.

So, don't hang around in the office. Look out of the window, not in the mirror. Get out there. And don't read planning blogs, and books…

UNDERSTANDING PEOPLE

2 minute checklist

o   Never lose touch with real people. Successful
    brands appeal to the masses.

o   Remember: you're not 'typical'. You're younger, better
    educated and earn more. You lead a busier life, work longer
    hours and watch less TV. Your consumption habits are not typical.

o   Never assume your audience is like you. And don't assume they
    share your interests. You work in an industry obsessed with what's
    changing – what's new and fashionable.

o   Always note first thoughts on a brand when starting work on it.
    You're still not 'typical', but it's at this point when you most closely
    mirror what real people think of the brand or category.

o   Find ways to break out of your bubble and see the world from your
    audience's point of view. Get out more. Don't rely on social media.
    Remember: 80% of adults *don't use* Twitter.

o   Consciously expose yourself to contrasting points of view. Read the
    Sun AND the *Financial Times*. Buy the *Angling Times* or *Saga Magazine*.
    It's more useful than reading a planning blog.

o   Delve into the data. What do people earn? How do they spend it?
    What do they do with their time? Some numbers may surprise you.

o   Remember: around 85% of life still takes place
    offline. Digital data is useful, but it is only a part of
    the picture. Complement it with 'old school' survey data,
    like TGI.

o   Don't rely on quick-and-dirty staff surveys. You need properly
    designed research, with big, unbiased samples. And that costs
    money.

o   Fight to get face-to-face contact with people who buy and use your
    brand. If not formal research, there are other ways. Go where they
    go. Do what they do. Take your earphones out and listen. Eat your
    lunch on a park bench and watch people.

o   Get on a bus. Shop at Lidl. Hang around in McDonald's. Listen to
    Jeremy Vine, not just the *Today* programme.

o   Get out of London. Remember: 'Middle England' is where your
    clients make their money. Not Hoxton.

HOW UNDERSTANDING MEN HELPED REGAIN BRAND LEADERSHIP
FOSTER'S

Useful case study

Every successful beer brand has intimately understood their male drinkers, and built communication around this understanding. However, back in 2010, Foster's had lost touch with a new generation of men. Life had moved on for blokes, in ways that weren't all positive. But Foster's, like other beer advertisers, had failed to spot what was changing for their 'Tribal Drinkers'.

A simple idea to help understand these men better revealed something interesting…

These so-called Tribal Drinkers – men 18–30ish – had been typically characterised as blokes living for Friday and Saturday nights when, fuelled by banter and spontaneous fun, in-jokes not insecurities were the order of the day.

But the planners had a breakthrough when they gave bartenders in pubs 'eavesdropping duties'. They asked them to listen in to their customers' conversations and keep a diary of what blokes were *really* talking about to each other.

Although superficially young men had seemed pretty happy with their lives, this eavesdropping by the publicans discovered a very different picture.

Modern life was getting tougher for young men. They faced many dilemmas. How could they ever afford to leave home? Should they get serious with a girlfriend?

How could they compete with the prowess on display in pornography? And what about performance at work?

Our Foster's guys were more 'Troubled Drinkers' than 'Tribal Drinkers'. Their superficially larky get-togethers were actually a coping mechanism. Amidst all the banter, mates were acting as support group and sounding board for dealing with life's issues. Humour helped soothe each other's insecurities and diffuse the awkwardness around them.

This new understanding became the foundation for the Brad and Dan 'Good Call' campaign. Here, British blokes called Aussie 'agony aunts' Brad and Dan to get their advice on their everyday worries. For example, Warren from Halifax asked: 'My girlfriend's new haircut doesn't suit her. Should I tell her?' The campaign took Foster's back to brand leadership, and won the Grand Prix IPA Effectiveness Award in 2014.

OLDER PEOPLE ARE ~~NOT~~ BIG SPENDERS

'How many marketers does it take to change a light bulb? The answer is
"Millennials". Because the answer to every fucking question
in marketing is "Millennials"'
Mark Ritson

When we started in advertising, the 'Grey Consumer' was a hot topic. The proportion of older people in the population had begun to rise. Many were surprisingly affluent. These trends were forecast to accelerate as the 'Baby Boomers' turned into 'Empty Nesters'. Soon we'd all be chasing the 'Grey Pound', forecasters told us.

But fast-forward 30 years, and we're more obsessed with youth than ever. Those demographic forecasters weren't wrong. The proportion of young people has indeed fallen. And the proportion of older people has increased in most developed markets: in the UK today, the over-45s outnumber 16–24-year-olds by around four to one. These over-45s are more affluent too, accounting for more than 50% of consumer spending and an even larger share of wealth. And these proportions keep climbing.

Young people, however, are having a tougher time. Debt, soaring housing costs and high unemployment or 'under'-employment mean young people in developed economies have less money to spend. And the last recession hit them particularly hard. So, as the experts predicted, the real money now increasingly lies with older people. Why then are we still obsessed with youth?

'Get 'em young' the logic goes, and you keep them for life. This is true for some categories, such as bank accounts. Here, switching is still rare. But in most categories, brand switching is too frequent to justify such a long-term approach. Even car-makers find it hard to justify focusing on younger drivers, despite high sales values and long purchase cycles.

The second argument for focusing on Millennials is their difference. They consume different media. Live different lives. And have different brand relationships. Conventional advertising won't cut it here, supposedly. However, this can all be exaggerated. While young people do, for example, spend less time with TV and radio than older people, traditional channels still account for over half of their media day.

Next, it's argued that Millennials represent the future. What they do now, everyone will be doing one day. This is probably the weakest argument of all. Our job is to sell to society as it is now. Not as it will be in 10 years' time. Young people change behaviour as they grow older, so they're not always a reliable guide to the future. We need to distinguish 'life-stage effects' from 'cohort effects'. Just because young people watch less TV than average, TV viewing is not necessarily bound to decline in the future. Young people have *always* watched less TV than older

viewers. It's because they go out more.

We suspect that advertising's obsession with youth is partly due to lack of perspective. We all tend to assume the average person is someone like us. And people who work in advertising are mostly young. Now there's less TGI analysis and fewer focus groups going on, young planners are often disbelieving of how old the people buying their brands actually are (TGI reveals, for example, that the average new car buyer in the UK is 56).

But maybe there's something else going on. We all admire the energy and creativity of youth. Youth is sexy, fun and interesting. Ageing, on the other hand, is embarrassing, unattractive and a bit scary. Perhaps the real reason we ignore demographic realities is because they remind too many of us of our own mortality. This could explain why the people who bang on most about Millennials are usually way past 30.

Perhaps Millennials themselves, far enough from mortality to fear it less, could lead the way in intelligently addressing the needs of the people who really have the money these days?

GRANDPARENTS ~~DON'T~~ HAVE POTENTIAL

'The agency business has demographically cleansed itself
of mature people'
Bob Hoffman

A few months ago, we were talking to some people in qualitative research groups about family holidays. The respondents were moaning about the industry practice of raising prices when the kids were off school. They talked about the difficulties of taking time off work to cover the long summer holiday weeks. They swapped ideas about keeping the children entertained on a budget.

Nothing surprising there you might think. But there was. Because these women and men weren't parents. They were grandparents. And as they chatted, it became clear that a sea-change is occurring under our marketing noses. But it's one that seems to have slipped the notice of many of us charged with understanding the world we live in.

We do seem to have belatedly caught up with the idea that men do housework. We know they shop for (and cook) food. And as evidenced by 'dad and child' ads, we also realise dads now look after kids.

But when it comes to grandparents, where are they all? When did you last see grandparents in a marketing plan? When did you last write about grandparents in a creative brief? When are the modern grandparents in advertising?

The facts regarding this silent tidal wave of grandparental change are startling.

Cast aside your stereotypes of grandpas with walking sticks and grandmas knitting.

In the UK, while the average age of having a first child rises, the age of becoming a first-time grandparent is falling – to around 50 years now. One in five people in the UK is a grandparent. And will be so for 35 years (compared with 14 years as an adult with no children, and 22 years as a parent with a child living at home). The number of UK grandparents will increase by a quarter by 2020… by which time one in three people will be one. Far from sitting around knitting or doing crosswords, 23% of UK grandparents are currently in full-time employment.

The story is the same around the developed world. There are 65 million grandparents in the US (growing at twice the rate of the US population as a whole). And they fit their jobs and lives round serious amounts of childcare to help their sons and daughters to go to work. Not surprisingly, this trend has increased sharply since the last recession. One in 14 US children now lives in households headed by their grandparents. Nearly 1 million are raised solely by their grandparents. Apparently, children's playgrounds now feature at some US retirement complexes, reflecting this new reality.

Across Europe, we see the same pattern: 40% of grandparents in 11 European countries now provide regular childcare for their offspring's children.

Employed, active and often with more disposable income (and time) than parents, this new breed of grandparent represents an untapped opportunity for brands ranging from food and children's health to holidays. Why, then, has our industry closed its eyes to this sweeping demographic shift affecting the lives of millions of potential customers?

Maybe it's another manifestation of our preoccupation with youth. Perhaps it reflects a sense that demographics are somehow 'old school' now? (In our early careers, demographic trends were planning bread and butter; strategy documents regularly started with demographic influences on a market.) Or maybe it's simply another casualty of today's preoccupation with new digital opportunities, blinding us to structural changes in our societies (although grandparents are of course very active online too, but that's another myth to bust…).

THINKING ABOUT DEMOGRAPHICS

2 minute checklist

o   Understand who buys your brand. Tailor your
    strategy, tone and media plan to your audience.

o   Don't dismiss demographics as 'old school'. Age, income
    and education are still massive influences on buying.

o   Don't just trust your intuitions – look at the data. Remember:
    you are not typical.

o   Don't just look at digital sources. Many are biased demographically.
    'Old school' sources such as TGI are more reliable. They have
    representative samples.

o   Challenge received wisdom about Generation X-style social groups.
    A lot of it is bullshit. Know your demographic facts.

o   Don't obsess over Millennials. There's little empirical evidence they hold
    different attitudes. And at less than 10% of Western populations, and
    with a lower proportion of disposable income, you'd be right to
    question the extent of their presence on briefs.

o   Don't underestimate the potential of the 'Grey Market'. Older people
    outnumber Millennials, have more cash, and more time to spend it.
    The bigger the price tag, the more important they are.

o Understand the difference between 'life-stage effects' and 'cohort effects'. Young people buy fewer cars than older people. That doesn't mean their generation is abandoning cars (a cohort effect). It's just that cars are expensive. Young people can't afford them yet (a life-stage effect).

o Don't fall for stereotypes. Demographic groupings conceal lots of variation. Some Millennials like knitting. Some retired people go to the gym. Being a grandparent in your 40s isn't unusual.

o 'Older' people are particularly varied: 60-year-olds are different from 80-year-olds. Healthy 80-year-olds are different from frail ones. And spending power varies enormously, because of cumulative effects of saving.

o Don't assume you have to show your target demographic in the ad (see Chapter 8). That's not how ads work.

THESE ARE ~~NOT~~ THE GOOD OLD DAYS

'While it's easy to lie with statistics. It's even easier to lie without them'
Frederick Mosteller

Marketing and advertising people can talk a load of nonsense at the best of times. But if you want to hear them at their worst, ask them to talk about social trends. The average social trends presentation is a guaranteed mix of the obvious, irrelevant and false.

Recently, we were listening to a conference speech about 'changing lifestyles'. Life nowadays is faster than ever, said the speaker. We work longer hours. We have less free time. Families are fragmenting. Food is eaten on the run…

We've been listening to this bullshit for 30 years. And it's no more true now that it was then. The inconvenient, less headline-worthy truth is that people have *more* free time than ever. Economic cycles wax and wane, but the long-term trend in all developed economies is toward shorter, more flexible working hours. And longer holidays. People start work later in life and spend much longer in retirement. Work takes up a smaller percentage of our life than it used to.

Related myths about pressures on family time are equally false. Contrary to popular belief, in developed economies parents spend *more* time with their children these days. Not less. Research shows the amount of time families spend eating together has stayed remarkably constant over the years. As has the amount of time they spend together watching TV.

The idea that the pace of life is spiralling out of control is not new. Alvin Toffler used it as the basis of his bestselling book *Future Shock*. Nineteenth-century writers such as Friedrich Engels bemoaned the death of traditional family life. Even Socrates complained about the shocking manners of the youth. No matter what age we live in it seems, the past was always a slower, gentler time.

So why do we cling to this distorted view of the past? Why does life feel like it's always getting faster?

Part of the answer lies in the way we experience and remember our own lives. As we go through our careers, most of us do get busier. We become more productive. We work faster. We take on more responsibilities, at work and at home. Our own pace of life does get faster. But that doesn't mean that life in general is getting faster. It's us who're changing. Not society.

This effect is compounded by the flawed nature of memory. The hazy way we remember the past makes it seem less busy. And the tendency to remember positive experiences more than negative ones gives it a rose-tinted glow.

This personal tendency toward nostalgia is then fuelled by media. News stories about society focus on change. And negative stories sell more papers than positive ones. Read the *Daily Mail* for long enough, and you too will be convinced the world's going to the dogs.

But perhaps the most intriguing explanation for this kind of nostalgia is that it reflects our concerns and desires. We feel harried and stressed, not because we have less free time, but because we feel, or are told, it's important to get the most out that time, and increasing affluence gives us lots more options. We fret about spending 'quality time' with our loved ones, not because we do it less, but because we prize it more, now basic needs are largely fulfilled. For anyone who wants to understand human behaviour, this is interesting stuff.

So next time some social commentator harks back to a golden age when life was slower, simpler and happier, with no evidence to support their view, remember that this tells you more about our society's values than our behaviour.

PEOPLE ~~NO LONGER~~ READ BOOKS

'Death, in marketing terms, rarely comes'
Mark Ritson

Returning to work after the festive season, we were comparing our children's respective Christmas present lists. We noticed something surprising. Between us, we have three offspring, ranging from six to 21 years of age. And on all their wish-lists, alongside the stuff you'd expect modern kids to want – clothes, money and electronic gadgets – there were lots of books. Not e-books. Real, paper books.

And what was noticeable was that the kids all spent lots of time reading these old-fashioned books over the holidays. Not because they had to – there were plenty of other electronic options – but because they wanted to. The six-year-old even spent New Year's Eve reading a book from the public library, of all things, ignoring her pile of new Christmas presents.

Aren't books supposed to be dead? Don't kids spend all their time Snapchatting and flicking through Instagram instead? It seems not. On New Year's Day, Les had the odd experience of being the lone family member Facebooking while the rest of the family were engrossed in books.

But surely young people don't turn real paper pages anymore? Aren't they all using their Kindles and tablets? No again, it seems. Gran loves her Kindle (large print is helpful), but the kids seem to love the feel of a real book. And before you ask, we don't have particularly weird children. Look at the stats. According to Nielsen, sales of e-books have been declining for a couple of years now. Real books are bouncing back. In particular, e-books have lost ground in young adult fiction, the publishing success story of 2014. *Girl Online*, the debut novel by internet star Zoella, sold more than 78,000 hardbacks in its first week – beating all the *Harry Potter* and *Twilight* books.

Far from killing books off, the digital revolution is giving them a new lease of life. Electronic publishing lowers barriers to entry for new authors. But the really successful ones then make the jump to 'real' book publishing – *Fifty Shades of Grey* anyone? Movies of books in turn sell more books – notice all those teenagers reading *The Hunger Games* on the bus a while back? Rather than distracting young people from books, social media encourages them to read: book blogging is popular and teenagers love following favourite authors on Twitter. A Voxburner survey for *The Bookseller* magazine recently reported that 49% of readers aged between 16 and 24 had joined a fan group, website or Facebook group related to a book, and 40% followed an author on Twitter. Seventy-five per cent said they preferred print books over e-books.

There's a wider truth here. Whenever radical new technology emerges, we always assume it will kill the old stuff.

Radio was supposed to kill the gramophone in the 1920s. But recent years have seen a vinyl resurgence. TV was supposed to kill radio in the 1950s, but people still listen to radio an average of two hours a day. The internet was supposed to have killed TV, but people still watch nearly four hours of TV a day.

Old and new technologies do compete with each other. Just as different species do. Sometimes new technology does make the old one extinct. But more often, the two find different niches, or even work in symbiosis. So Twitter and Facebook have enhanced, not replaced, TV, with the big TV reality events thriving in a state of mutual benefit, with viewers commenting on social media. And smartphones and tablets haven't killed TV advertising. Instead, they've made it work harder. We can search product info, watch ads again, check deals and buy advertised products online.

Trend-spotters and futurologists should have learnt by now. More exciting new tech will come our way. Yes, our world changes very fast, but old tech can be surprisingly resilient… like books.

THE OLD STUFF DOES ~~NOT~~ MATTER

'Since things in motion sooner catch the eye than what not stirs'
William Shakespeare

We attended a conference run by Thinkbox (the UK body responsible for TV advertising) a few years back. An interesting session at the end gave useful facts on the current state of the UK TV market.

One headline struck us as particularly fascinating: 90% of all TV programmes are still watched live.

Consider how much TV technology has changed, and this is quite remarkable. Despite on-demand viewing, digital recording and the range of devices 'TV' is now viewed on, people still mostly choose to watch TV in the old-fashioned way – live.

However, the next day's headline in the *Financial Times* told a different story. 'Rise of TV on-demand poses ad challenge. Tenth of viewings now time-shifted,' it thundered. A quarter page of copy outlined this brave new world of time-shifted TV, completely ignoring the '90% still live' story.

We've come across this 'silent majority' syndrome before. Around 80% of shopping is still done in real shops. Around 80% of media is still consumed offline. And around 80% of 'word of mouth' conversations are still spoken – on phones, or yes, even face to face. Yet in each case, we tend to focus on the 20% that's online.

Why is this? There seem to us to be several reasons.

First, we focus on what's easy to see and measure. Online, it's easy for us to track and record what people watch, say, do and buy. It's much easier to measure sentiment on Twitter or Facebook than in the local pub. It's easier to track visits to a website than footfall in a shop.

But the easy availability of online data can distract from the bigger issue of what quietly continues to go on in the 'real' world. Just as 95% of the universe is dark matter and dark energy that can't be seen, 80% of the marketing universe is behaviour that can't easily be tracked. So we concentrate on the 20% that's visible.

Secondly, it's human nature for our eyes to alight on movement not stillness. We ignore what Sherlock Holmes called 'the curious incident of the dog in the night-time,' ie the dogs that don't bark in the night. Some 90% of people who visit a social site don't post anything. We focus on the 10% who do. Futurologists and journalists are culprits here, since their raison d'être is to highlight what's new and changing.

Thirdly, because we're marketing and communication people, we're different from the majority. In the US and UK, we're less than 1% of the population. We tend to be younger. Richer. Better educated. Without kids. And we live in a handful of big cities. So it's all too easy for us to overlook how different our lifestyles and perceptions are from the people we talk to.

We overlook the reality that 83% of UK new car buyers are over 40. We're surprised to learn that scrapbooking in the US is a $4 billion industry – with more participants than golf. We've no idea that sewing and crocheting in the UK are more popular than video games. Yet we've never come across a reference to scrapbooking or sewing in a meeting or a brief.

Here's our advice. The next time you see a percentage in a headline, subtract it from 100%. Spend a bit more time thinking about the larger number. Because that may just be where the opportunity is.

THINKING ABOUT TRENDS

2 minute checklist

o   Beware sloppy thinking about social change.
    Look for the facts before you believe the headlines.

o   Don't confuse how you feel *your* life is changing with
    how society in general is changing. There may be no
    relation between them (remember life-stage vs cohort effects).

o   Approach trends presentations with scepticism. Trend-spotters
    need new stories to sell. Get the data that supports the story.

o   Don't trust journalists either. Remember the old journalist's rule:
    three stories is a trend.

o   Don't overestimate the pace of social change. Even professional
    forecasters get this wrong.

o   Always go back to data. Be familiar with the key economic and demographic
    trends that underpin most other changes in society.

o   Remember the words of sci-fi author William Gibson: 'The future is already
    here, it's just not evenly distributed'. Society rarely changes en masse. New
    ideas and habits take time to spread. Old ones often hang around until the
    previous generation dies off.

o   Take the long view. Big trends operate over decades, not years.

o   Trends presentations focus on what's changing. The bigger story may be
    what isn't. This doesn't make such great headlines, but is more
    important for strategy.

TREND SPOTTING

A useful tool

While working on this book, a young planner came to ask about food trends. He wanted to look at the rise of more 'natural' diets: vegetarianism, veganism, organic food, that kind of thing. It quickly became apparent that he thought this was something that had emerged over the last couple of years.

Five minutes with Google Ngram Viewer gave him a more long-term perspective. This free online tool allows you to see how often a word or phrase appeared in published books, going back to 1500. It's a great way to get a sense of broad cultural trends. For example, the chart below suggests that vegetarianism is an idea with a very long pedigree, which is now being gradually replaced by more sophisticated forms of 'clean eating', such as veganism and organic food.

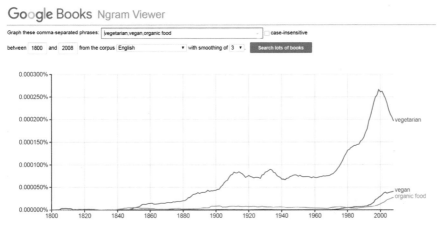

Source: http://books.google.com/ngrams

Notes:

_____

_____

_____

_____

_____

_____

_____

_____

BUDGETS
AND MEDIA

'Content without reach is like building cathedrals in the desert'

Hamish Priest

SEVEN

INTRODUCTION

In this chapter we turn to how much we spend on communication, and where we choose to spend it. This is another area where ungrounded assumptions and wishful thinking result in bad planning and reduced effectiveness.

We're constantly told that media rules have changed (Oreo Super Bowl tweet you have a lot to answer for…). But the basics still stand. To have even a chance of moving the dial, you need big numbers of people to see what you're doing. Our first article, then, looks at the importance of reach, and how to build it in today's media landscape.

In our second article we consider something that worries people about reach: the idea of 'wasted' budget. But a look at how advertising works in both the long and short term reveals how,

far from wastage being a bad thing, it's positively vital for long-term brand health.

That leads naturally to the question of budget. In today's world of low-cost (or even 'free') digital media and 'zero-based budgeting', clients are increasingly unwilling to open their wallets. But, as our third article shows, you get what you pay for. When it comes to advertising effectiveness, there's no such thing as a free lunch.

Finally, we look at media choice. We explode the myth that TV is dying, and show how changing viewing habits are making TV advertising more, not less, important for brand growth. To counter the nonsense, you'll find some evidence-based tips for choosing media in the digital age.

REACH ~~NO LONGER~~ MATTERS

'We targeted too much, and we went too narrow'
Marc Pritchard, P&G

One night in the pub, a digital planner was talking about her campaign. We asked how many people it reached. 'Reach?' she sneered, 'it's not about reach anymore.'

Really? But this is a common view these days. In the old days, goes the argument, you needed big audiences. These days, communications are more targeted, interactive and engaging – so reach no longer matters.

It's a seductive idea. Agencies like it, because it allows them to experiment. Clients like it, because it appears to save money. Unfortunately, it's bollocks.

Logically, there are just two ways to get a big payback from a small audience. Either you get them to spend a lot, or they must encourage others to do so.

Neither is a sure-fire route to success.

The first strategy is to go for 'brand loyalty'. Target some segment of the market, then extract as much value from them as possible. But data shows that loyalty strategies rarely work. As we discussed earlier, the main driver of brand growth is penetration.

The second strategy is to go for 'influence'. Spend your money cleverly on targeting a few people, often 'opinion leaders'. Get them to influence other people for free. They in turn influence others, until you get a chain reaction. Eventually you reach the 'tipping point'. This can happen. Fashions often propagate in this way. So do playground crazes. When texting took off, its success took mobile companies by surprise.

But this sort of chain reaction is rare, and hard to predict. It only happens if people are connected in the right way, and if the behaviour in question is highly 'infectious'. In this respect, toys and fashion are unusual: consumption is visible and interesting. But this isn't true in most markets. As we've said before, people don't care much about most brands.

Social media data might seem to contradict this. Coca-Cola has over 100 million fans globally on Facebook. That seems a hell of a lot of brand engagement. But Coke has around 4 billion users worldwide. So those Facebook fans represent a tiny percentage of users. And the figures look similar for other big brands. We estimate that for the most popular brands on Facebook, only one in 20,000 sales actually leads to someone 'liking' the brand.

And it rarely goes further than that. Facebook's own data reveals that less than 1% of those 'fans' actually talk about the brand. These numbers are far too small to create the big effects marketers need.

Duncan Watts, a principal research scientist at Yahoo!, concludes that it's impossible to reliably generate large effects by targeting a few key influencers.

Rather, the optimum strategy is to use mass marketing. Then let viral propagation take the message further. Exponential effects are rare, 'But you can double your impact, which is still pretty good,' Watts says.

The same is true offline. Famous campaigns get people talking and amplify the message. IPA data suggests this amplification can double effectiveness. But you still need good reach in the first place.

That's why Share of Voice (SOV, a measure of paid-for exposure) correlates more closely with Share of Market (SOM) than online 'buzz' (the free amplification). In fact, research suggests that the effect of SOV on sales hasn't changed much in 30 years. Despite the digital revolution, reach still matters.

Smart marketers like Coca-Cola understand this. For them, social media are a clever way to make mass marketing work harder. But companies that rely too heavily on viral propagation are taking a risk, as Pepsi found out to its cost with its ill-fated social media 'Refresh Project'. So the dream of 'target and get the rest for free' unfortunately remains just that – we still need to put our money where the mouths are.

REACH

2 minute checklist

o   Always aim to get more customers, from all segments of the market. It's the main way brands grow.

o   Talk to everyone who buys your category. Talk to them regularly; advertising memories fade.

o   Build and maintain 'mental availability' (share of mind). Make sure your brand comes to mind easily; evokes rich associations; feels familiar; seems the 'natural choice'.

o   Try to get more exposure than your competitors. Share of exposure means share of mind.

o   Don't get seduced by the lure of a free lunch. 'Owned' and 'earned' media amplify effects, but rarely work well without 'paid' media. Make sure your budget is big enough.

o   Go for reach, rather than frequency. Reach as many category buyers as possible.

o   Avoid repeatedly hitting the same people. It yields diminishing returns.

o   Keep frequency under control as you build reach. If using digital media, cap frequency directly. Otherwise control frequency by spreading activity across the year.

o   Understand your brand's seasonality, and
    plan around it. All markets are seasonal to some
    extent.

o   If seasonality is weak (eg loo roll), aim for year-round
    presence.

o   If seasonality is strong (eg Christmas trees), focus advertising on
    the buying season.

o   Remember: media prices are seasonal too. Avoid expensive times
    of year if you can.

o   Use econometrics to optimise trade-offs between reach, frequency,
    seasonality and media costs.

MEDIA CONSUMPTION

A useful tool

Assessing the strengths and weaknesses of various media channels is hard for non-specialists. There are so many options to choose from now. Different media report different metrics, making it hard to compare. And intuitions are skewed by our atypical media habits.

For the beleaguered planner trying to get a sense of proportion, the IPA TouchPoints survey is a useful corrective. Based on a mobile panel, TouchPoints collects detailed data on media consumption from a representative sample of adults, in the UK and US. Different media are measured on a like-for-like basis, allowing direct comparison. And while access to the full dataset requires a subscription, there's useful free stuff available at www.ipa.co.uk/touchpoints.

The chart below shows UK 2017 data. Traditional media like TV, Outdoor and radio still dominate reach and dwell time. Adults watched over 3.5 hours of TV a day on average; 85% of that was live on a TV set. The pattern is similar for Millennials: they consume less of all media, but TV and Outdoor still top the charts.

This is not what we've been led to believe. We're told everyone's watching stuff on Netflix, YouTube and Facebook. But the data shows that, while subscriber VOD (Video on Demand) and other forms of online video are gaining ground, people spend relatively little time with these channels. And a lot of online viewing is incremental – in bed, on the train, at work. Traditional TV viewing – on the box, in the living room – has not been affected very much so far.

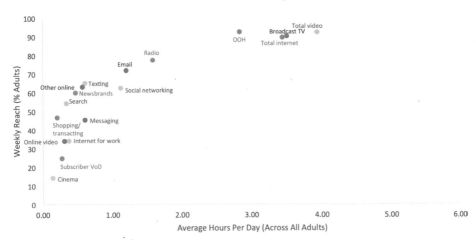

The media landscape in 2017

Source: IPA TouchPoints

WASTE IS ~~NOT~~ GOOD

'The waste in advertising is the part that works'
Tim Ambler

It may or may not have been Lord Leverhulme who started it, but whoever it was, the demon of 'wastage' has long stalked media and budget discussions. 'Wastage' crops up frequently – usually in support of efficiency of online activity compared with TV.

To quote from a recent contributor to *Admap*: 'Online media, pound for pound, is cheaper and more cost effective than traditional media models based on largesse, waste and inefficiency.'

Bullshit. This is one of those dangerous situations where choice of word puts an instant, but erroneous, value judgement on a fact. How can 'wastage' be a good thing? But there's plenty of evidence to show that waste in advertising is often the bit that works.

Narrowly targeted media have a seductive illusion of cost efficiency. But trying to reduce 'wastage' can make your marketing *less* efficient. Here's a concrete example. A while back, a client questioned why we were using TV advertising to support his brand, when only half the audience was in the target market. Surely it would be better to use a more targeted medium, like Direct Mail (DM)?

Well, no, it wouldn't, on simple cost grounds. In that particular case, we found it cost 92p to talk to someone in our target audience with DM, but only 3p to talk to them on TV. Even though half our TV advertising was 'wasted'.

Sometimes, this apparent wastage isn't wastage at all. The effects of advertising aren't always immediate. And they aren't always direct. When Volkswagen runs a TV ad, it knows most of the audience aren't about to buy a new car. But many will buy one in the future. And research shows it's a good investment to start talking to them now. And if they like 'the VW one with the singing dog', talk about it or pass it on to their friends online, that's not wasted money either. Great ads create ripple effects that go way beyond the original audience.

Really great ads go even further. They change the way a whole society feels about a brand or an issue. This matters because, in most categories, people's brand choices are hugely influenced by what people around them think. If you're buying nasal hair removers, you probably don't much care what other people think about the brand you choose. But publicly bought and used brands (clothes, beer, newspapers, cars, credit cards, baby food... ie most brands) derive much of their value and meaning from what people outside the category think about them.

People who buy Mercedes and Prada do so because everyone knows what those brands stand for, even if they're not the 'target market' themselves. To create these shared cultural meanings,

we need people outside our target to overhear our communication. In other words, we need wastage.

Finally, conspicuous wastage itself can be a sign of quality. Biologists find that apparently 'wasteful' displays – elaborate antlers or extravagant tail feathers – can lead to evolutionary success. They signal health and fitness to potential mates. Similarly, apparently 'wasteful' communication (high comparative spend on media, production values or, post-Cadbury's 'Gorilla', minimal product focus) has been shown to lead to business success by signalling quality and credibility to potential customers.

This is especially true when there's little functional difference between brands – which is often. As Tim Ambler puts it: 'Conspicuous waste... promotes an inclination to purchase a product by reinforcing – quite apart from the advertisement's informational content – impressions of a brand's quality.'

Or, put more simply by a customer when Virgin Media started using sprinter Usain Bolt in its ads: 'They must be doing well to use him'.

So don't forget: waste is good.

WASTE

2 minute checklist

o   Don't confuse effectiveness with efficiency. Effectiveness is the extent to which you've achieved your goals. Efficiency is a measure of effort needed to meet them.

o   Focus on effectiveness first, efficiency second.

o   Pay most attention to the effectiveness metrics. These are the big, absolute numbers: numbers of people reached or recruited, net sales or profit generated etc.

o   Don't get too hung up on efficiency metrics. These tend to be ratios: cost per exposure, cost per recruit, return on investment etc.

o   Never use efficiency metrics to set budgets. Diminishing returns mean that the easiest way to increase efficiency is to cut budgets. Leading to falling sales and profits.

o   Don't target too narrowly. It may be efficient, but it's rarely effective. Tight targeting means low sales and profit.

o   Check that the benefits of targeting outweigh costs. Highly targeted media are often expensive.

o   For immediate sales activation, target people
    who're likely to buy the category now or soon.

o   But for longer term brand building, go broader. Talk to
    anyone who may buy in the next couple of years.

o   Think how to influence people's social networks. Buyers
    are influenced by the people around them.

o   Aim for fame, if you can. Get people talking and sharing.
    Get coverage in the media. Famous advertising can be highly
    effective *and* efficient.

o   Don't be too afraid of 'waste'. Doing something big and expensive
    can be effective in its own right. It can signal that your brand is thriving,
    popular and profitable (the 'Peacock's Tail effect').

BUDGETS DO ~~NOT~~ MATTER

'Invariably the individually precise is culturally invisible'
Chris Binns, MediaCom

Last summer, we were given a task by a big multinational: could we review their research and look for insights to help them grow market share? We read a mountain of material – everything from packaging semiotics to obscure product usage in emerging markets. But something was missing. In over 2,500 pages of research, there was only one mention of marketing budgets. Just one.

This is symptomatic of a trend. People obsess about brand architecture, purpose, or the content of their communications. But budgets get remarkably little attention.

Why is this? Agencies may be less interested in budgets now they're not paid on commission. Clients often have to work within budgets outside their control. The constant drive for efficiency (rather than effectiveness) has made cutting budgets a point of honour – encouraged further by digital evangelists, the most extreme of whom advocate cutting 'paid' media spend to zero.

But budgets still matter. To understand why, let's remember some inconvenient truths about advertising.

As Ehrenberg and Sharp have shown, the single most important factor driving brand preference is 'mental availability': how well known a brand is, and how easily it comes to mind. Brands with low mental availability tend to struggle, rejected in favour of more familiar rivals. Or not considered in the first place. Brands with high mental availability don't have to push so hard to sell, so tend to have higher market shares and better margins.

Building mental availability means constantly reminding people of your existence. What you say and how you say it are important, of course. But the most important thing is just to be out there. Psychologists call it the 'mere exposure effect': any kind of exposure to a brand increases propensity to buy. As Ehrenberg said, advertising is about publicity, not persuasion.

And don't focus on one segment of the market. Successful brands build high mental availability among all users of the category. This requires many, many exposures. Econometric studies routinely show that number of exposures is a crucial determinant of effectiveness. There are diminishing returns, so reach is more important than frequency. But generally, the more exposures you get, the more you sell.

Strong brands are built through millions of exposures over many years. 'Owned' and 'earned' media rarely deliver enough exposures to do this job on their own. Unless your brand is exceptionally interesting, few people will beat a path to your owned media without prompting. You may occasionally get

lucky and have a one-off viral hit, but few brands are capable of repeating this. The notable exceptions are brands like HuffPost or BuzzFeed that devote huge resources to producing interesting content, every day.

As someone wise once said, 'Content without reach is like building cathedrals in the desert'. For most of us, promoting brands that ordinary people don't find interesting, 'paid' media is still the only reliable way to get that reach. For this reason, budget is crucial. Research shows that, all other things being equal, a brand's market share tends to follow its Share of Voice (SOV) in paid media. And that doesn't seem to be changing. Evidence from the IPA Databank suggests that the influence of paid SOV is increasing, not decreasing.

Creativity, clever media planning and technology can make budgets go much further, of course. But the best cathedral in the world will stay empty if the budget is too small.

SETTING BUDGETS

2 minute checklist

- o Remember: marketing is largely a numbers game. Effective campaigns need to reach lots of people; many not in the market now.
- o Don't think you can get the reach and scale required without paid media.
- o Face facts. Budgets still matter. Great creative work and clever media planning makes budgets go further. But generally, the more you spend, the more effective your campaign.
- o Don't allow budgets to be determined by history or politics. Think carefully about what's required to meet your business objectives.
- o 'Zero-based budgeting' is good discipline here. But bear in mind that you need to include a budget to *maintain* existing demand.
- o Familiarise yourself with simple budget-setting techniques like advertising-to-sales ratios and SOV (see graph overleaf).
- o For more sophisticated budget setting, use econometrics.
- o Don't use ROI to set budgets – that always leads to cuts. Aim to maximise *net profit*, not ROI.

o   Then, *for a given budget level*, allocate budgets
    to maximise ROI.
o   Budget for the long term, not just the launch phase.
o   Don't panic when your sales eventually plateau.
    That's normal. Advertising is now *maintaining* sales.
o   Be aware: if you cut the ad budget, sales will fall — and
    the damage can be hard to reverse.
o   Remind budget holders that two years without ads is enough
    to kill a brand, if competitors take advantage of the opportunity.

BUDGETING FOR GROWTH
VOLKSWAGEN

Useful case study

The 1980s was a successful time for Volkswagen UK, with strong sales of the iconic VW Golf. But by the early 1990s, VW was beginning to lose market share. We were asked to find out why.

Our first step was to look at the relationship between Share of Market (SOM) and Share of Voice (SOV). Decades of research in many different categories has shown there is a general relationship between a brand's SOV and its SOM. All things being equal, brands that set SOV above SOM tend to grow, while those that let SOV slip below SOM tend to go into decline.

How share of voice affects growth

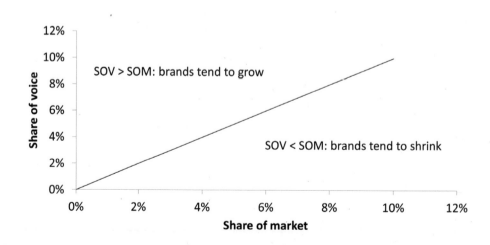

Our analysis quickly revealed that part of VW's problem was lack of investment. Volkswagen's SOV was way below the level required to maintain market share; indeed, they had the lowest SOV of any continental car manufacturer.

The following year, Volkswagen doubled their advertising budget, taking SOV back into the growth zone. The results, published in a series of IPA Effectiveness papers, were remarkable. Sales responded immediately, and continued to grow steadily for years after. Market share more than doubled. Econometrics showed that, in the first eight years alone, increased adspend generated £2 billion worth of extra sales.

Who says budget doesn't matter?

Source: Society of Motor Manufacturers and Traders

TV IS ~~NO LONGER~~ EFFECTIVE

'TV isn't dying. It's having babies'
Bob Hoffman

If there's one thing marketers all seem to agree on, it's the death throes of 'traditional' TV advertising. Type 'TV advertising is dying' into Google, and thousands of articles emerge. All explaining why TV is doomed in today's digital world.

For a start, TV viewing's in terminal decline, isn't it? Families no longer sit in front of the TV every night. Instead, they entertain themselves with a growing list of personal alternatives: phones, iPads, Facebook and computer games.

And the dwindling pool of TV viewers is fragmenting as channel numbers increase. So the number of people reached by any given TV spot goes down and down each year. And if TV advertising can no longer reach mass audiences, surely it loses its raison d'être? And isn't it obvious that all this will get worse? It's accepted wisdom that young people hardly watch TV anymore. And the rise of PVRs and Netflix means those who do watch telly are avoiding ads. TV advertising is doomed.

It's a simple argument. And like most simple arguments, it's completely wrong. Unfortunately for the doomsters, the facts point in the opposite direction. Start with the assumption that TV viewing is in decline – hardly ever questioned, but totally lacking in evidence. Total TV viewing is actually rising in many countries, including some with the most technologically sophisticated consumers in the world: total US TV viewing increased 16% over the 10 years to 2010. Why has this trend largely gone unnoticed? Because while total TV viewing has been rising, pundits have focused instead on ratings for individual channels and programmes – both falling as the number of channels grows.

On to the doomsters' second assumption: audience fragmentation is a 'bad thing for TV advertisers'. The argument here goes that because each TV spot reaches fewer people, TV advertising no longer reaches mass audiences. But this argument ignores price. With the explosion of TV channels, spot prices have plunged, increasing the number of people any given TV budget reaches. Yes, more spots are required. But TV ads still reach people en masse, And it's increasingly cheap to do so. In fact, channel fragmentation helps TV advertisers in two ways: more competition drives down the costs of reaching people with TV, and a wider range of content enables tighter targeting. So TV becomes increasingly efficient at reaching people.

This helps explain another inconvenient truth. Most marketers assume TV is becoming less effective. Yet the numbers stubbornly disagree. Great TV campaigns still generate high levels of awareness. Still get talked about by the public. And still yield big financial paybacks. IPA Databank figures suggest that the sales effects of TV advertising are getting bigger, not smaller.

But what about the future? If young people are turning away from TV, surely things look bleak? Wrong again. Teenagers do watch less TV than adults. But they always have. Because they go out more. When they're home, TV is still an important part of their leisure time.

OK, but what about ad avoidance? If people are skipping ad breaks, why should advertisers bother with TV? This sounds like a killer argument. Until you look at the facts. PVRs do increase ad avoidance a bit. But the effect is much smaller than initially feared. And people with PVRs end up watching a lot more TV, offsetting effects of ad skipping. So PVRs may end up increasing the reach of TV advertising.

The effects of online video channels have been similarly mixed. Ad-free channels such as Netflix are growing fast. But they still account for a relatively small percentage of people's viewing, much of which is actually incremental. And if they want to start making a profit, they may have to start carrying advertising at some point. As YouTube already does.

In 2004, one agency chief said that, 'in 10 years' time, there won't be any such thing as TV advertising'. He was clearly wrong. If anything, the digital revolution has made TV advertising even sharper and more efficient. TV advertising will continue to change. But anyone betting on its imminent death needs to take a long cool look at the facts.

MEDIA CHOICE

2 minute checklist

o   Fit the medium to the task.

o   Remember the two main tasks for any marketing campaign: brand building and sales activation.

o   Allocate around 60% of comms budget to brand building, 40% to sales activation. Flex this to suit your category and brand.

o   Understand which media are better for brand building, and which are better for activation.

o   For activation, use targeted media. Talk to people who are buying now, or very soon.

o   Choose information-rich media to send these people relevant messages and information.

o   Don't waste time entertaining or seducing. Activation is about efficiency. Make it quick and easy to buy. Include a direct response mechanism. One-click ordering is the paradigm.

o   Digital channels are ideal for activation. They're tightly targeted, information-rich and responsive. Paid search is probably *the* activation medium now, with email and programmatic advertising.

o   For brand building, choose broad-reach media.
    Talk to everyone who might buy the category in
    the next two or three years.

o   Understand which media build reach quickly.
    Offline media do this job best, but digital channels
    can help, especially for younger audiences.

o   Choose emotive media for brand building. Pictures work
    better than words, and video works even better. Music plays
    an important role.

o   Don't dismiss TV advertising. It reaches lots of people, stirs their
    emotions, and gets them talking. It's still the most powerful brand
    medium we have.

o   Use online video to complement TV. It extends reach and allows
    people to share your ads.

Notes:

_____

_____

_____

_____

_____

_____

_____

CREATIVE WORK

'The greatest danger for most of us is not that our aim is too high and we miss it, but that it is too low and we reach it'

Michelangelo

EIGHT

INTRODUCTION

We turn now to what gets us all out of bed in the morning: the great creative work that works.

We start by looking at what's creatively important for success. The 'System 1' way that ads work means people respond to ads as a whole – not just to a 'message'. In fact, often not *even* to a message. Messages are less important than we think.

The second article looks at a creative tenet many planners have been brought up on – that ideas need to be 'relevant'. This thinking still lies at the heart of a lot of research. But what does relevance mean? How important is it?

We're often challenged on an idea's 'ownability'. In the third article, we discuss what we really need to 'own'.

People don't take brands seriously. Neither should we when it comes to advertising. The fourth article looks at the power of humour.

Because ads work as a whole, 'System 1' details, often seemingly small ones, matter more than many realise. The next article explores this and the implications for pre-testing.

The sixth article turns to music. It's hard to argue the financial case for a great track. But research shows music is one of the most important and underrated investments we make in the effectiveness of campaigns.

We then look at casting issues. The seventh article discusses watch-outs with 'real people', while the next considers the value of flaws. Some clients believe we need to show the target audience in the ad. But do we? In the ninth article we show this isn't how ads work.

The next two articles turn to the issue of creative consistency. When do we really need to change campaign idea? What do we keep, and what change?

Finally, we discuss something the ad industry has always intuitively believed (and now we have evidence for it): creativity makes a big difference to effectiveness and efficiency.

IT'S THE IDEA AND ~~NOT~~ THE EXECUTION THAT MATTERS

'A great ad is 80% idea and 80% execution'
John Hegarty

In a recent meeting, discussion turned to the issue of creativity. What exactly was the role of creativity for brands? How could it add value?

This was a big, complex question. But interestingly, the same words kept cropping up. It was clear that, to many people, creativity was about being new and different.

It's a common view, but it got us thinking. Maybe creativity isn't really just about new ideas. Maybe it's not about ideas at all. There's another side to creativity. Less frequently mentioned, but possibly more powerful. Brilliant, effective creativity can be less a function of how new and different an idea is, and more about how the idea is brought to life.

We sometimes forget that people respond to the design of a pack or a website or an ad as a whole – not just as an idea, a message or a storyline. Just as when we watch a stand-up comic we respond to the whole person – their posture, face, physique, timing, accent, gestures, eye movements – long before they start to tell the joke.

As Bill Bernbach said: 'Most readers don't come away from their reading with a clear, precise, detailed registration of its contents on their minds, but, rather, with a vague, misty idea, formed as much by the pace, the proportions, the music of the writing as by the literal words themselves.'

Craft, artistry, execution – call it what

you will. It's a very different thing from the need to communicate a message. Or even to showcase a big, new creative idea. Yet it's incredibly powerful.

Studies by Paul Watzlawick on relationships show that what he calls the 'meta-communication', or *how* something is said (gestures, tone of voice, body language etc), is far more influential than the 'message', or *what* is said.

It is the fine, very often apparently inconsequential, details that matter. Not just the big idea. It's the frog leaping into the coloured balls in the Sony Bravia ad; the eye-patch in the classic Hathaway Shirts ads; the Smash Martians' laughter; the Russian accent of Aleksandr the meerkat; Moz the monster's fart from under the bed. It's what Bernbach referred to when he wrote: 'I can put down on a page a picture of a man crying and it's just a picture of a man crying. Or I can put him down in such a way as to make you want to cry. The difference is artistry – the intangible thing that business distrusts.'

Business distrusts art because it's obscure, complex and ambiguous. But the critic William Empson believed ambiguity was the essence of poetry; hiding the message made it richer. And that stuff matters for very practical reasons. 'Doing the common thing uncommonly well' gets more attention and stimulates more mental processing. It creates more and deeper mental connections. Gets a bigger emotional response. And is more likely to be remembered. It's also more likely to be talked about and shared. People share kitten videos not because cute kittens are a new idea, but because of the ways those kittens are being cute.

Without this magic, even the best new 'creative idea' will fail. Evidence from Peter Field and Millward Brown themselves shows that creative awards correlate with effectiveness better than pre-test scores. But with this magic, ads without simple 'messages' can have big effects. It's hard to sum up simply the 'messages' or ideas of Nike's 'Write the Future', or Budweiser's 'Whassup?' But they pay back in spades.

HOW CREATIVITY ADDS VALUE

2 minute checklist

o   Your great strategy and idea isn't enough.
    Execution is where the magic happens.

o   Never underestimate the importance of creativity.
    Great creative can make your budget work 10 times harder.

o   Understand how your ads will work. Are they 'System 1' or
    'System 2' ads? (See 'System' breakout box in Chapter 3.) The
    role for creativity is different.

o   For a System 1 ad, don't fuss about explicit messages or rational
    persuasion. Use creativity to evoke feelings and create associations to
    influence people in less conscious, rational ways. These may not 'make
    sense', rationally.

o   For a System 2 ad, use creativity to highlight product, brand and
    message. Not distract from them. Simple messages work best.

o   Don't think 'emotion' in 'System 1' ads means making people cry or
    laugh out loud. The feelings involved may be more low key.

o   And don't think System 2 persuasion is *totally* rational. Emotions and
    feelings are central to all human decisions. Learn a persuasion lesson
    from the great orators: the way you say it is as important as
    what you say.

o   Always aim for creative work that's utterly
     distinctive, and immediately recognisable as your
     brand's. Regardless of how your ads work, branding is
     always important. But branding is more than the logo.

o   Don't think creativity is just about innovation. Sometimes
     innovation is important. System 2 ads may focus on 'new news'.
     A completely new idea can also get a strong System 1 response.

o   But sometimes it's just as effective to 'do the common thing
     uncommonly well'.

IF IT'S NOT RELEVANT, IT CANNOT BE EFFECTIVE

'We have to entertain in order to educate, because the other way round doesn't work'
Walt Disney

Many years ago, we worked on Dulux. Dulux ads have always featured a shaggy Old English Sheepdog. They still do. The dog appears as a branding device alongside the pack shot. Or during the ads, typically padding through newly painted sitting rooms. Back then, Dulux made so many ads that they tested them all using their own in-house pre-test. One standard question was: 'Why do you think there is a dog in this ad?'

We always felt rather sorry for the research respondents. How exactly were they meant to reply? There wasn't any good answer. Other than 'because there always has been a dog in Dulux ads'. In fact, there wasn't any obvious reason for the dog to be there. The story goes that, once on a Dulux ad shoot, an Old English Sheepdog belonging to a crew member wandered onto the set. It looked good, so the dog was kept in. The rest is history.

Which brings us to relevance. Many of us were raised on a mantra that ads needed to be distinctive and relevant. But how important really is relevance? The many successful, but 'irrelevant', advertising campaign ideas around (from Russian meerkats to a *Dirty Dancing* Skeletor and He-Man) make us wonder if we overestimate the relevance of relevance.

Being 'relevant' may mean sacrificing more important things in an ad. Ads must be interesting because people have busy lives that don't revolve around brands.

Paint isn't especially interesting. But dogs are. Ads must be emotional, because that's what sells best, especially over the long term. Paint isn't particularly emotive. But dogs are. Ads need to be branded on some level, and that's hard if they're not distinctive. If Dulux's ad had just focused on paint, it would have looked like any other paint ad. But the dog made it distinctive.

So, by making Dulux ads more interesting, emotive and distinctive, the dog made them more memorable. This is a general phenomenon. Experiments have shown it's easier to remember messages when they're accompanied by unrelated, 'irrelevant' video footage. All this helps explain why some of today's most effective ads seem based on 'irrelevant' ideas.

Over time, of course, what at first seems 'irrelevant' can become relevant; eventually the shaggy dog in the ad (and in fact the entire breed) became instantly recognisable as 'the Dulux dog'.

But does that mean we can put *anything* in our ads? Not quite. We believe ads do need to be 'relevant', in two deeper senses.

First, they need to be relevant to people's lives. As Bernbach said: 'A communicator must be concerned with the unchanging man – what compulsions drive him, what instincts dominate his every action.' Paint is pretty peripheral to most people's lives most of the time, but pet dogs have deep associations with hearth, home and family – themes that are universal and unchanging (and not unrelated to paint).

Secondly, when you tap into these universal motivations, you tend to generate big emotions, which can be very helpful. But it's important to generate the *right* emotions. We need some 'emotional relevance'.

Citroën once ran an ad featuring supermodel Claudia Schiffer taking her clothes off. They generated either lust or anger, depending on your point of view. But neither emotion was relevant to choosing a car. Contrast that with a more recent Volkswagen ad, where the Dad gives a Polo car to his daughter as she leaves home. That generated protective feelings that have always been part of Polo's positioning.

Maybe therein lies the answer to that tricky Dulux pre-test question: 'The dog's in the ad because he's a relevant irrelevance'.

RELEVANCE

2 minute checklist

o   You need relevance, in the broadest sense.
Connect your brand and category to me, my goals
and my interests. But remember: there are different
ways to be relevant.

o   Close to the point of purchase or use, 'connect' with relevant
messages (activation) – eg product features and benefits,
prices etc.

o   Or connect to the media context: a sale offer on Black Friday,
a digital poster featuring a Cornetto, thermally activated on a hot day.

o   At other times, 'connect' with more universal interests and concerns
(brand building). Remember: most of the time, people aren't interested
in brands or products.

o   Don't think you need a USP. Effective advertising often 'owns the generic'.

o   Don't bother dancing on strategic pin-heads trying to find a 'relevant'
minor product difference. An 'irrelevant' but distinctive product
'truth' like the round Tetley tea bag is still a relevant connection
for creative ideas to jump off from.

o   Don't assume you need a relevant *message* at all. Advertising
can work by creating 'System 1' connections too. 'You're so
Moneysupermarket' connects the brand to a relevant

feeling: triumph at getting a cracking deal.

'Have a break, have a Kit Kat' connects the brand to a relevant consumption moment.

o But do connect your brand to the category, and the context in which it's bought/used.

o Be wary of emotive or 'lifestyle' ads that aren't tethered to the category. Some brands can get away with this – 'Gorilla' didn't mention chocolate. But most brands can't.

o Be especially careful with 'Purpose' ads. Great, 'relevant' feelings connected to my ideals and interests. But what's it got to do with beer? Or conditioners?

o Always connect your ads firmly to your brand. Make everything you do distinctive.

o Don't be too obsessed with relevance. Irrelevant details can be powerful. Think 'The Man in the Hathaway Shirt's' eye-patch.

o Create relevance through repetition – think of the Dulux dog.

WE CANNOT OWN THAT

'It takes 10 years to establish a clear position in the market, and most brands never get close because a procession of different marketing directors and advertising agencies arrive and stamp their own idiosyncratic and entirely inappropriate personal "vision" onto the brand'
Mark Ritson

Here we go again, we thought. Clients eagerly anticipate the unveiling of a new campaign idea. Slow smiles. They really like it. It will stand out brilliantly. They don't even mind that we're not showing the target audience in the ad.

But then we show our end-line, which sums up the campaign idea and would be used across all our communications. They seem to like that too… at first. Then the moment's pause. And then that question: 'But can't anyone say that?'

It's interesting how often this question crops up. And it's interesting, too, how little it's challenged and picked apart to understand the false thinking behind

it. What does it mean for an end-line (or any other brand property) to be 'ownable'?

Well, one way for a brand to 'own' an end-line might be to include the brand name itself – as a pun, a rhyme or some play on words. Castlemaine's 'Australians wouldn't give a XXXX for anything else' comes to mind. But these are rare. And seem to be getting rarer. Perhaps partly because they don't translate well, and so can't easily be used in global campaigns. Maybe, like jingles, it's more of a fashion thing.

Another way a brand might 'own' an end-line would be to base it around a product benefit – 'Domestos. Kills all known germs. Dead' was an example. But in a world where functional advantages are quickly matched by the competition, brands rarely own these claims for long. In fact, any bleach could make the same claim as Domestos.

And this takes us to the nub of how branding works. Brands succeed not by being different, but by being distinctive. Brands need a distinctive style, tone of voice and personality. They need to have their own way of saying what they do. An end-line's job is to sum that up in a memorable way.

Think about two great brand end-lines: Nike's 'Just do it' and Tesco's 'Every little helps'. There's nothing inherently ownable about these words. Or the sentiments behind them. You couldn't come up with a more ordinary bunch of words if you tried. But each of these lines reflects an attitude to the category in question that's clear, distinctive and memorable. And over time, they've become inextricably linked to the brands in question.

And that's the point. 'Ownership' takes time and money. The smart marketing directors who bought those successful long-running campaign ideas and end-lines weren't agonising over whether they were 'ownable'. Instead, they rolled up their sleeves, got behind them and set about owning them. That requires hard work, consistency, and yes, financial investment.

It's the same with our names. Anyone could be called Les Binet or Sarah Carter. But over time our names accrue meaning. And we grow to own them. So let's stop ducking responsibility. When next presented with a potential end-line, the right question isn't 'Is it own-able?', it's 'How can we own it?'

'CAN WE OWN IT?'

2 minute checklist

o   Don't assume ads need a USP they can 'own'. They don't.

o   Don't assume brands need to be functionally differentiated from competitors to 'own' some market segment. They don't.

o   If you do happen to have a significant functional 'ownable' advantage, shout about it. But remember, competitors will try to match you. So it probably won't last.

o   So why not 'own the generic'? Killing all known germs is a generic claim. But consistent use over decades means we associate it with Domestos.

o   Be distinctive and well-branded – that's more important than any 'ownable' claim. Pears' transparent soap has no obvious functional advantage over rivals. But it's utterly distinctive. And that sells.

o   Make everything your brand does distinctive and easily recognisable (even if the product isn't) – from ads to packaging. Create distinctive assets you can 'own'.

o   Don't dismiss distinctive and memorable slogans or catch phrases as 'old hat'. You may not know exactly what 'Vorsprung durch Technik' means in German. But you'll know it means Audi in the car market.

o   Find other ways to be distinctive, beyond
    end-lines. Brands can 'own' characters (the Lloyds
    black horse), music (British Airways), or even a running
    joke (Specsavers). Many memorable campaigns combine
    them (GoCompare).

o   'Own' distinctive assets in the legal sense. 'I'm Lovin' It' is a
    registered trademark.

o   Remember: to have real value, assets must be strongly associated
    with their brands. This 'ownership' is only achieved through consistent,
    repeated usage over years.

o   Create campaigns, not ads. Encourage clients to invest in them over
    the long term.

o   Don't worry too much if 'anyone could say that'. Say it differently. And
    keep saying it differently, then eventually you *will* own it.

THE EFFECTIVE GENERIC
CRAVENDALE MILK

Useful case study

Here's a nice little case study on the power of the generic benefit: IPA Effectiveness Gold Award-winner Cravendale milk.

Cravendale milk is filtered in a special way. This means it is 'purer', so stays fresher longer and tastes 'cleaner'.

The UK launch campaign used messaging focused on the superior purity and longer-lasting freshness of Cravendale – the things that made this milk different from your average pint. But the campaign bombed. (Research suggested this rational messaging made people suspicious of how a new milk might have been 'messed about with' to last this long.)

So a second campaign was produced. This introduced an enthusiastic spokesman, Mr Hinchcliffe, with literally a visual checklist of all Cravendale's superior selling points vs other milk – cleaner taste, purer, lasts longer – but this time adding in the reassurance of no artificial additives. This campaign did even worse. We'd just overloaded the ad with even more messages of how this new milk was different and, supposedly therefore, better.

In desperation, we changed tack. We junked the strategy of leading on all the rational differentiators and instead focused on what was essentially a generic benefit

– the great taste of Cravendale (with filtering relegated to just a 'reason to believe' in the voiceover). Now we were creatively liberated from all those 'how we're different messages'. So we were free to dramatise the generic great taste benefit in a funny, emotional, distinctive way. The ads were a kind of bovine Hitchcockian thriller, where sinister-looking cows were on a mission to get their Cravendale milk back… because it tasted so good. In short, leading on taste, not the differentiating messages.

And this time, the campaign worked brilliantly.

The moral: don't overlook the power of the generic.

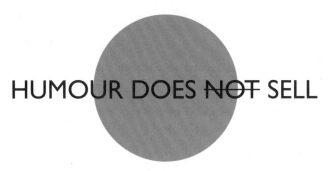

HUMOUR DOES ~~NOT~~ SELL

'A little nonsense now and then is relished by the wisest men'
Willy Wonka, 'Charlie and the Great Glass Elevator' (Roald Dahl)

Many years ago, we worked on a cracking new TV idea for Dulux paint. It showed people up and down Britain painting different rooms in their homes. All set to a stirring song. We were convinced we were on to a winner. But when we showed it to the client, we met an unexpected problem. One scene showed someone cheerfully painting their loo. The client was horrified: 'Dulux customers do not use the toilet,' she said frostily. The scene had to go.

We've always sympathised with clients when faced with new creative ideas to judge. Marketing is a serious business in the sense that it affects the financial wellbeing of companies, their owners and staff. Brands are serious and important in the sense that they're valuable financial assets. Unfortunately,

this leads some to believe all aspects of marketing must be done in a serious way. Their view echoes that of ad pioneer Claude Hopkins, who asserted in his seminal 1923 book, *Scientific Advertising*: 'Don't treat your subject lightly. Don't lessen respect for yourself or your article by any attempt at frivolity. People do not patronise a clown. An eccentric picture may do you serious damage. One may gain attention by wearing a fool's cap. But he would ruin his selling prospects.'

So, people become 'consumers', shopping becomes the 'path to purchase', and minor tweaks become 'major product innovations'. Brands that people kind of like but don't think about much become 'challengers' or 'icons' evoking trust, loyalty and deep devotion.

Agencies can be just as lacking in perspective. We can be equally precious about 'the creative process', 'digital customer journeys' and the like.

But does it matter if we take it all just a bit too seriously? We think it does.

Seriousness seriously inhibits creativity. We're at our most creative when we're in a relaxed, playful mood. There's a reason we have our best ideas lying in the bath. Why creative departments have those snooker tables. And why creative teams often come up with their best ideas when mucking about, saying something ridiculous, then thinking, 'hang on, that might actually be good'. If we want great creativity, we need to take a light-hearted and playful approach. Technology companies such as Google understand this well. But some more traditional marketers seem not to.

Excessive seriousness can make marketing less effective. There are times – usually just before we make a buying decision – when we want facts and figures to help us decide. At these times, a rational, no-nonsense approach tends to work best. But mostly, marketing works in a different way: creating emotional associations, so we feel good about brands when we encounter them again later. This kind of brand advertising needs to charm and seduce us. Not persuade us. And as with other sorts of seduction (note mentions of GSOH in dating profiles), playfulness and humour work rather well for brands. They disarm our critical faculties, creating warm feelings towards brands. Research shows it's those feelings that drive long-term ROI.

Advertising lacking charm can have the opposite effect. It raises our defences, so we scrutinise its claims more critically. It creates resentment, so even if we believe what's said, we feel hostile towards the brand. The net effect is poor sales and lower profits. Especially over the longer term.

To paraphrase Oscar Wilde: marketing's too important to be taken seriously.

HUMOUR, PLAYFULNESS AND CHARM

2 minute checklist

o   Don't take your brand too seriously. Being
    playful works.

o   Be like the parent pretending a spoon is an aeroplane,
    to coax their reluctant toddler to eat: disarm to persuade.

o   Don't think you need to be serious to convey a clear message
    – even a serious one (the 'Dumb Ways to Die' campaign
    for Metro trains in Australia).

o   Don't think you need to be serious to be credible. If people don't
    like your ads, they're less likely to believe what you say, no matter
    how well supported with RTBs. Likeable, charming ads are more likely
    to be believed.

o   Use humour to tackle things people find embarrassing or stressful –
    from death (Allied Dunbar's 'For the Life You Don't Yet Know') to
    incontinence ('Stirling Gravitas' for Tena Men).

o   Harness the 'halo effect'. When people like an ad, they tend to like the
    brand. Humour is a highly effective way to sell things, with or without
    messages.

o   Go for humour if you want fame. Funny
     ads make brands famous: people love to share
     jokes. From Marmite's 'Love/Hate' to Snickers' 'You're
     Not You When You're Hungry', many of the world's
     best-known campaigns are rooted in humour.
o   Be cautious about humour in activation work. People in
     active shopping mode may not want to be entertained. It
     may annoy them if you try. They're more likely to want
     information on product, price and how to buy it.
o   Know when to entertain, charm and seduce, and when to cut
     to the chase and sell. As with relevance, it's all about context.

THE POWER OF FUR

Useful observation

It's interesting to ponder why so many famous, highly effective campaigns involve furry animals: we've mentioned lots in this book – the meerkats, the Dulux dog, the Felix cat, the Andrex puppy, the Cadbury gorilla, the PG Tips chimps and now Monkey, John Lewis's Christmas ads featuring a bear and a hare, a boxer dog and a furry monster. There's no rational, serious or 'relevant' reason explaining why animals seem to sell so well.

But it's down to our 'System 1' brain and the way this works again (see the first article in Chapter 3). There's something deeply embedded in our psyche that responds peculiarly well to being sold to by animals. Like music, animals attract our attention, are enjoyable to watch, and invoke powerful positive emotions in us which attach to the brands involved and endure over time. It's no surprise that so many examples of long-running campaigns involve an animal.

Animals are salesmen we're more than happy to welcome into our homes and lives. Our 'Ah, but' 'System 2' critical faculties are neatly sidestepped by Mr and Mrs Bear as they journey through Heathrow, or Paddington bear as he dispenses M&S Christmas presents.

And animals have other advantages too. As legendary creative John Webster (the Honey Monster, George the Hofmeister bear, the Cresta bear) used to say: 'They don't age. They'll never molest children. And you've got them forever.'

The power of fur.

Notes:

_____

_____

_____

_____

_____

_____

_____

DETAILS DO ~~NOT~~ MATTER

'Great things are done by a series of small things brought together'
Vincent van Gogh

We attended a fascinating research debrief this year. The research compared two versions of the same TV ad. The brand was a health product. The advertising idea was a simple one. Each 'testimonial' ad showed someone who'd suffered from a health issue saying how they'd tackled the problem successfully using our brand. The ad was designed to inspire people by showing them someone they could relate to, who really had used our brand to solve the problem. The desired response was: 'If they can do it, so can I'.

The ads that went into testing were both finished films. They were identical in every way: same length, same script, same music, same narrative structure, same product sequence and so on. They differed only in the choice of the lead character.

The first ad featured an attractive middle-aged woman. This version failed in quantitative testing. People understood the ad well. They took out the product's health claim. And they logged the brand at high levels. But it totally failed to engage and inspire people. They showed no evidence of wanting to try the product themselves. 'Persuasion' was therefore low. Further analysis of their responses suggested there was a subtle problem with the female 'hero': she seemed just a little too happy and perfect. People couldn't put it into words easily. They just found her a bit hard to identify with, or believe she had the health issue we were talking about (although she did).

The second ad debriefed featured a middle-aged man as the hero. And the response was very different. Same understanding, same recall of the health claim, same levels of branding. But this time people found the ad inspiring and engaging, and felt that 'If he can do that, I can too'.

Close analysis revealed that this wasn't a gender issue – the health issue in question affects men and women equally. Rather, it was a subtle difference in personality that swung it. This guy was just a bit more down to earth and warm. Viewers of both sexes felt they could identify with him more.

This example illustrates brilliantly how, in the real world, subtle, seemingly irrelevant details, often hard to put into words, can have big effects on people's response to advertising. The traditional model of advertising assumes people process advertising messages in a rational way. And it's the persuasive power of those messages that determines whether they buy the product. But behavioural economics paints a different picture. Real people cruise along on autopilot, making most judgements and decisions at a semi-conscious level, based on heuristics. They react to characters in advertising on an intuitive, emotional level. And these gut reactions colour how they

process everything else. Psychologists call this the 'halo effect'. It means who says the words matters more than what they say.

This is just one example of a broader 'affect heuristic': positive emotional responses to individual executional details transfer to the advertised brand. So small changes in casting, lighting, photography, editing etc can be more important than advertising message. A good example is music choice. This usually has little to do with the rational content of an advertisement, but can improve ROI by 20–30%.

This has huge implications for research. If advertising is primarily about communicating ideas and messages, then animatics should be just as good for testing as finished films. And this is what we're routinely told. But if advertising effectiveness lies more in executional details, then animatics may not be good enough. It also raises interesting questions for us all about strategy and briefs. How do we plan for effective advertising when so much ROI power lies in the execution?

It seems that in advertising, as in so much of life, the devil is in the details.

MAGIC VS MESSAGES
THE IMPORTANCE OF DETAILS

2 minute checklist

o   Beware the 'message myth'. Some of the world's most effective ads have no discernible message at all.

o   Don't venerate the idea over the details. Small, seemingly irrelevant details can have a huge influence on effectiveness.

o   Think like a journalist. They're drilled to seek the specific 'telling detail' so their stories sing. This applies to ads too. Details matter.

o   Remember: we respond to communication as a whole. Not just as a message, idea or even storyline.

o   Think about the 'body language', not just the language. *How* something is said, or who says it, often matters more than *what* is said.

o   Be aware of the importance of casting, lighting, location, clothes, music, the 'vibe' and so on.

o   Think about implications for pre-testing and tracking. If most ads don't work by rational messages, subtle details matter, and these appear only in finished creative work – are you measuring the wrong things in the wrong way?

o   If you do need to pre-test, look for methodologies
    capable of probing less conscious, more emotional
    responses to the 'body language' of ads.
o   Pre-test finished ads, not animatics, wherever possible.
o   Always pre-test with the music you're going to use.
o   Recognise the flaws in proposition/message/concept testing.
    It only looks at language, not 'body language'.

MUSIC IS ~~NOT~~ SO IMPORTANT

'We're emotional creatures. We take in information through the heart – and that's where music goes in. That's what makes it so powerful'
John Hegarty

Recently, we were working on a pitch. A number of teams had come up with ideas which were being honed in the run-up to pitch day. The lead idea was a big emotional story about a family, set in a South American city. There was no dialogue. At the top of the script were the words, 'Music: suitably epic'. It was the day before the pitch when we realised 'Music: suitably epic' was still on that script. The specific music track hadn't been discussed at all. All the chat had been about the action.

We suspect this is common. We all know music matters. Around 90% of international TV ads use music. But it seems we don't think music matters that much. Hence ads go into research with a vague choice of track as the 'right kind of thing' to 'give a feel' for the

finished ad. Or a researched music track is swapped just before airing because of some legal issue or client cost concern.

Our disregard for the importance of music shows when we look at research literature. Of over 48,000 articles on the WARC database, only 10% of them mention music at all. Only 29 (less than 0.1%) discuss it in any detail. But the research that has been done on the effects of music suggests these are far greater than we seem to assume.

Research shows that music increases the attention paid to ads as well as recall of brand and message. We suspect these effects may be very long term. Think about the ads we remember word for word from childhood – it's highly likely they used music. (Jingles have become uncool nowadays – wrongly, in our opinion; they work really well.)

Because music works as an 'access all areas' pass to our 'System 1' brains, it's perhaps not surprising it has such powerful effects. Research on the implicit effects of advertising shows ads influence us in ways that may not involve explicit messages at all. And these more implicit, emotional approaches tend to have broad, long-term effects. As a result, this 'emotional priming' produces very large long-term sales effects and profits.

Music is really brilliant at creating these emotional reactions that attach directly to brands and make them more desirable. Research we've undertaken recently with Goldsmiths University in London shows how adding music to an ad increases implicit brand effect by around 11%.

What about effects beyond the individual? Advertising and brands work in a social context. People watch TV ads together, and sometimes they talk about them, or share them with friends. These social ripples massively increase communication effectiveness. And from Moneysupermarket to John Lewis, it's striking how often music is central to these famous campaigns. It's estimated that the free media exposure arising from the music in John Lewis's Christmas ad each year increases campaign impact by around 75%.

Given all this, it's perhaps not surprising that the IPA Databank shows that TV ads using music prominently are significantly more effective than ads that don't, enhancing effectiveness by 20–30%.

So, over a fifth of the effect of an ad may come from its music – meaning choice of music can easily determine whether or not the ad pays for itself.

That's too important to leave to the last minute.

MUSIC

2 minute checklist

o   Understand the power of music. It's one of those 'details that matter'.

o   Understand the various ways music works.

o   Use music to make ads more enjoyable. Remember: liking is the single best predictor of ad effectiveness.

o   Use music to stimulate emotion. Emotional associations have big impacts on long-term brand preference.

o   Use music to get additional exposure, through media coverage, radio airplay and online sharing. Music is a great way to make your ads famous.

o   Want memorability? Music helps. We remember music easily, often for years. We can all sing ad jingles from our childhood. Use it as a distinctive asset brands can 'own' long term.

o   Pay more attention to music. Remind your clients that research shows music can boost sales effects by 20–30%.

o   Don't let conventional research fool you into underestimating the power of music. It's not easy to measure the effects of music with traditional questionnaires.

o Use research methodologies which pick up
music's implicit emotional effects. A typical 5-point
rating scale of 'I like the music' on a pre-test
questionnaire fails to do justice to music's importance.

o *Always* test ads with the music track you actually want to use.

o Invest time, money and energy to get the track you want.
Music is too important to be an afterthought.

o Think investment, not cost. Remember: the right music track
can easily determine whether your ad pays for itself.

MUSIC MAKES ADS MORE EFFECTIVE

Useful chart

	Number of cases	% cases reporting any very large business effects	Average number of very large business effects reported
Musical ads	21	93%	2.5
Other ads	142	73%	2.3
Difference		+28%	+20%

Source: IPA Databank 2008–2012

Notes:

_____

_____

_____

_____

_____

_____

_____

_____

HOW ~~NOT~~ TO USE REAL PEOPLE

'Humankind cannot bear very much reality'
TS Eliot

Recently, we attended an advertising research debrief for a 'functional food' brand. This kind of brand is rare because the product had a real and valuable functional benefit: it was scientifically proven to 'correct' a common medical issue. The campaign featured real people who'd used this brand, talking enthusiastically about how well it had worked for them.

In theory, the campaign should have worked a treat. Social psychology theory repeatedly describes the power of recommendation by 'people like us'. People in focus groups often suggest that using real people like themselves in ads helps them relate to the ads and believe ads' claims. And we all know about the phenomenal success of 'reality TV'.

But, you've guessed it. Our research debrief reported that the benefit communication came through loud and clear. The idea clearly worked well to inform people about this product and what it did. But unfortunately, it didn't work very well to persuade people to try the brand. Why was this?

The first clue may lie in what's happened to reality TV. When *Big Brother* started back in 2000, it was a pioneering social experiment which did feature quite 'real' ordinary people. The novelty TV format was intriguing. Viewing figures were huge. We watched it ourselves. But a decade or more later, the novelty has worn off. Nowadays any semblance of featuring real, ordinary people in reality TV has long gone. The Kardashians anyone?

The problem is that ordinary isn't really very interesting. And that matters. People don't watch TV to get information about brands and products. They watch to relax, be entertained and chill out with loved ones. They're not interested in brands — even when these brands really do work. So, if we're to stand any chance of making an impression, we have to be interesting.

And the trouble with ordinary people is, as our research brutally reminded us, they can just be a bit too… well, ordinary. Our campaign made the mistake of thinking that all a powerful rational message needed was testimonials from real people to persuade other real people. It rarely is though. Informing is not the same as persuading.

Persuasion is primarily emotional. Rational messages play a secondary role. Recommendations from friends and family can be influential, because we have an emotional bond with these people. But recommendations from strangers are processed in a more nuanced way. On TV, they're often screened out. After all, your real may not be my real. And even if it is my real, most people don't want their own, rather dreary reality reflected back to them when they settle down on the sofa after a hard day. Jim the cabbie or Pat at her yoga class may have had

success when they used this brand. They may be real and convincing. But are we interested? Does it emotionally move us at all?

Online, recommendations can have a lot of influence, but only for people who're already interested in the product, and close to buying it. Even then, people have become canny at sorting out which recommendations to trust and which to ignore.

So, can we ever use real people in our ads? And if so, how?

Maybe those Kardashians give us a clue. There are many examples of powerful creative work showing real people. But usually they're wrapped in an emotional context which makes them far from ordinary. The Paralympic athletes in Channel 4's *Meet the Superhumans* or the Sapeurs of Congo in the Guinness campaign were real — but far from ordinary.

Maybe TS Eliot was right. In advertising, as in life, humankind cannot bear very much reality.

IMPERFECTION IS ~~NOT~~ ATTRACTIVE

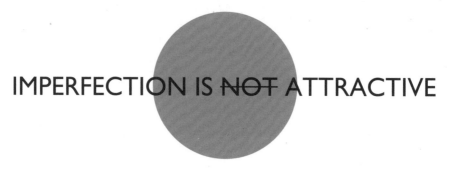

Kintsugi ('golden joinery'):
ancient Japanese art of repairing pottery with gold lacquer to celebrate flaws

Some years ago, we found ourselves in a heated debate. We were casting the hero of a new beer campaign, and the argument centred on what he should look like. The client was adamant the hero should be a bronzed beach Adonis with an impressive six-pack and just-enough facial hair. Weren't blokes all wanting to look like that these days? The creative team had other ideas. Their preferred bloke looked like he'd be great company to have a beer with. But Adonis he wasn't; more James Corden than James Bond.

We agreed with the creatives. Throughout history, from Odysseus to Princess Diana to Sheriff Woody, all the great archetypical heroes have had 'lovable flaws' which draw us to them. Our heroes aren't perfect – but they're more strong, engaging and alluring because of it.

A look at politics on both sides of the Atlantic shows the power of imperfection too. On the right, we have Donald Trump and Boris Johnson, whose gaffes, flaws and transgressions seem only to enhance their popularity among supporters. And on the left, we've seen the popularity of Bernie Sanders and Jeremy Corbyn – grey-haired, somewhat crumpled figures seeming to hark back to another era. On paper, none of them should stand a chance. But their flaws seem to make them more, not less, appealing to their followers.

So, can imperfection be a source of strength? And if so, why?

Imperfection attracts attention. In a world of identikit models, Kate Moss's crooked teeth and Cara Delevingne's strong eyebrows got them noticed, and remembered.

Imperfection signals authenticity. Compared with the previous generation of slick, PR-savvy career politicians, characters like Trump and Corbyn seem refreshingly honest (to their supporters at least), and therefore more trustworthy.

Flaws create empathy. People who are flawed seem more like us, and so more likeable. The impact of Nigel Farage – the beer-swilling, cigarette-smoking former head of UKIP – owed a lot to his carefully crafted 'ordinary bloke' image.

And finally, imperfection can be aesthetically pleasing in its own right, as the success of Dove with its 'Campaign for Real Beauty' shows. The Japanese even have a word for this – wabi-sabi – a view that celebrates the allure of the imperfect and incomplete. The wobbly line, the cracked leather, the faded patina – all draw, rather than repel, us.

Standout, empathy, attractiveness and trust – these are all qualities that define successful brands. So maybe it's time for brand owners to embrace the power of imperfection.

There are advertisers that get this, and their 'bravery' is rewarded by more powerful communications than their perfect 'everyone looks awesome' adland competitors. Think of the overweight construction worker pole-dancer (Moneysupermarket), Southern Comfort's 'Whatever's Comfortable' beach hero, or the sweating women in 'This Girl Can'. Their imperfections draw us to them. The brands feel more authentic. And we trust them more because of it.

So where are the 'flaws' in the personality descriptors that we craft for our brand definitions? We seem terrified to consider them – tying ourselves up in knots and qualifications to avoid any chinks of vulnerability or imperfection. 'Aspirational yet accessible', 'Strong but warm' – we've all written them.

Back to that casting session. Who won the argument? Adonis or flawed hero? Well the creatives got their man. The campaign worked brilliantly. Remember: imperfection sells. Our heroes are heroes because of their imperfections. Not in spite of them.

HOW ~~NOT~~ TO PORTRAY YOUR TARGET AUDIENCE

'You don't have to be black to identify with Othello. Just jealous'
Jeremy Bullmore

We were discussing a creative idea for a food brand the other day. The brand manager was unhappy. Volume potential lay in encouraging family usage. So he was worried that the proposed script showed a young, childless couple tucking into food with friends. A classic example of the 'identification myth', ie to appeal to certain people, we should feature these people in our comms. The result: heated debate at script and casting meetings. And ads featuring the ad-world's version of 'normal people who use the brand' – people almost like us, but with better hair, make-up and fridge cleanliness.

Showing the people you're targeting seems like common sense. So, what's the problem? Well, first, people don't really like seeing themselves in ads, whatever they say in pre-testing. Ask people in research who should feature in ads targeting them, and they tend to say 'people like us'. But that doesn't mean we should do it. As we saw in Chapter 4, M&S found this out to its cost some years ago, when it ran a TV ad featuring a naked 'ordinary' woman, mirroring the size and shape of most of M&S's customers. One City analyst memorably described it as 'the fat-bird-running-up-the-hill ad'. It didn't take long for this foray into 'real people' to be replaced by a successful new campaign featuring Twiggy, Dannii Minogue et al.

If you want to portray the public, warts and all, it's often best to do it at one step removed. Animal characters, for example, are fantastic for this. For 40 years, the famous PG Tips tea ads featured chimps dressed as humans, displaying all manner of snobbery, ignorance and intolerance to hilarious effect. Real people wouldn't have been nearly so funny, nor likeable.

The bigger reason why this 'my consumer should be in the ads' concern is unfounded is that people don't identify with what people look like; instead, they identify with their hopes, problems and challenges. It's why Shakespeare's plays are still so relevant today. As JWT's legendary Jeremy Bullmore put it: 'You don't have to be black to identify with Othello. Just jealous.'

A few years ago, we worked on an ad for British Meat. This featured a sweet old couple in their 80s celebrating their wedding anniversary with a steak dinner. It turned out to be by far the most successful ad of the long-running campaign – on every level, from tracking to sales. Young people loved it even more than older people. You didn't need to be aged 80 to 'identify' with the couple. Instead, everyone identified with the emotions of achieving and celebrating a lifelong, happy marriage.

Why was *The King's Speech* such a successful film? Not because we're all kings. Or have speech impediments. Colin Firth doesn't look remotely like King George VI. Instead, we all identify with the emotional themes: social exclusion, shame and the challenge of overcoming obstacles with the support of a friend. When people in research suggest that an ad's characters should be more 'like them', it's usually a symptom of a wider problem: the communication not resonating emotionally. Not identifying

with the casting is just a convenient, post-rationalised thing for people to say.

You might be wondering about the Dove 'Campaign for Real Beauty' at this point. This, of course, was Unilever using 'real women' in a very successful campaign. Is this an exception to the 'identification myth'? Talking to the planner involved, it seems not. Although the idea did feature 'real women' (albeit shot by an amazing photographer), the key to the campaign's success was still the way it worked emotionally. Women didn't love the 'realistic' portrayal of 'women like me' so much as what the campaign stood for – the idea that every woman has her own beauty – and the attack on the distortions of the beauty industry. The 'real women' in the ads were primarily shorthand for this bigger thought.

So what seems to happen is that the people we feature signal things about our brand, not our users. Yorkie (a chunky chocolate bar) typically featured blokes driving juggernauts in its ads. When it launched a new campaign with the line 'It's not for girls', female journalists sniped. But sales increased. And sales increased as much among women, who wanted a chunky chocolate bar, as men. The *brand* was manly, not necessarily the eater.

When you next find yourself debating the people in your ad, remember Othello.

WHO'S IN THE AD

2 minute checklist

o Help clients understand the importance of great casting. It can enhance stand-out, empathy, trust and aesthetic appeal. Get it right, and ads are more believable, distinctive and memorable.

o Be aware of how exquisitely sensitive our reactions to other humans are. Cast people who evoke empathy and stir feelings. These emotions are the key to effective brand building.

o Be careful when researching casting. Casting effects mostly work at the 'System 1' level, so are hard to pick up with traditional research.

o Don't believe people when they say they want to see themselves in the ads. Evidence suggests they really don't.

o Pay more attention to whether people can *feel* themselves in the ads. We identify with the emotions, not the person.

o Make your heroes 'credible'. But this doesn't imply simplistic realism. Actors or cartoon characters are sometimes more 'authentic' than real people.

o Avoid the bland, default and conventional – whether you use 'real people' or actors. Use casting to make your ads distinctive and memorable.

o Be sensitive about diversity and stereotyping. Things are changing. But we've a long way to go.

o   Be aware that marketers (in our experience) in less
    developed markets tend to be more conservative. But
    their buyers are often more open to change than they think.

o   Beware of stand-out and brand confusion issues if you use 'real
    people'. Once they were unusual in ads. Now they're common.

o   If you're going to show real people, do it in an interesting, distinctive
    way. The Halifax campaign mixing real-life employees with cartoon
    characters like Top Cat is a great example.

o   Remember: there's a reason why the best films and TV programmes
    don't feature 'ordinary people'. People prefer watching 'extraordinary
    people'.

o   Embrace 'flaws': the 'bigger than usual' nose of the Axe hero in 'Find
    Your Magic'; the non-identical eyes of the Guinness Surfer.
    Small things make a big difference. And get noticed.

o   Think how to address these important 'small details' in pre-test
    situations. It will be hard in an animatic.

CONSISTENCY ~~NO LONGER~~ MATTERS

'I have learned that any old fool can write a bad ad, but that it takes a genius to keep his hands off a good one'
Leo Burnett

2019 marks 30 years since the Felix cat food campaign first appeared on UK TV. Created by our agency back in 1989, it's since run consistently across the UK and Europe. Hundreds of executions, across multiple media. Launching new products and supporting old ones. All featuring the now-famous black and white cat on everything from posters to tea towels.

Felix has only ever had this campaign. Few campaigns anywhere in the world have run continuously for so long. But like the advertising jingle, the long-running campaign now seems a bit of an oddity. This is bizarre really. Clients rarely ask for campaign ideas that will need changing quite soon.

So why are long-running campaigns becoming so rare? On the surface,

it seems to result from managers acting responsibly: wanting to keep brands fresh and avoid 'wear-out'. The 'disruption' orthodoxy claims brands need to be in a state of 'continuous revolution' in order to survive.

But in reality, the desire for change usually has more to do with egos than responsible brand stewardship. It's long been a truism that marketing and agency people get fed up with campaigns long before real people do. Changing your campaign is a quick and easy way for managers to make their mark. 'Brand X stays with long-running campaign' is never going to make front-page news. One of the hardest marketing skills to master is the art of leaving well alone.

But does all this chopping and changing

do any harm? We think it does. No-one's arguing for the continuation of ineffective campaigns. Or for running the same execution for years. But there's evidence to suggest that, once a winning formula is found, advertisers should stick with it. Campaigns, even individual executions, take much longer to wear out than often feared. Having studied decades of econometric analysis on the subject, one major advertiser recently concluded that the idea of wear-out is a myth.

Recent thinking on how advertising works shows the importance of continuity and consistency, rather than disruption. It's clear that the old persuasion model is flawed. Most effective advertising works by building emotive associations at a less conscious level. This takes time and, above all, consistency. So new communication builds on what's gone before.

So a relentless pursuit of novelty leads to money wasted. Advertisers spend precious management time developing new ideas. And ROIs fall as people are subjected to a flurry of inconsistent campaigns. Our econometric work on Felix showed the advertising becoming more, not less, effective over time. That's the virtue of consistency.

The design industry seems to understand this better than we do. The Museum of Brands, Packaging and Advertising in London showcases the careful evolution of pack designs for great brands like Hovis or Persil over more than 100 years – each new design subtly building on the last. Always balancing consistency with the need for design refreshment.

There are sound neuroscientific reasons for this sensitive approach. Think of brands as well-trodden paths of neural connections that help us make buying decisions more efficiently, with minimal mental effort. We disrupt these associations at our peril, as the Tropicana US pack redesign flop showed.

When long-standing elements of the pack design were changed, sales fell fast as people found it harder to spot Tropicana on-shelf. A design volte face swiftly ensued.

We spend lots of time thinking about the relationship of 'consumers' with the brands they choose. We spend less time thinking about our own relationship with the brands we're responsible for. The best brand custodians are like the best parents: they know the value of consistency.

OLD ADS DO ~~NOT~~ WORK

'We all know that brand properties we inherit are much less valuable than brand properties we create: there's never been an exception to this curious truth'
Jeremy Bullmore

We were briefed on a new campaign the other day. But we couldn't understand why. The campaign to be replaced had only run at modest weights. Early indications showed positive sales effects. Why change so soon? We started thinking about this common dilemma: when to try something new, and when to continue building on what you've got.

Clients and agencies have powerful urges to make new work. Partly, it's self-interest: clients make their name from new work. And agencies do too. Partly, it's a kind of restlessness: we all tire of our ads years before the public. But mostly it stems from a genuine concern about 'wear-out'. If people stop responding to communications,

we're wasting money. If people start getting annoyed by it, then we might end up damaging brands.

But is wear-out really this common?

Most ads don't get much chance to wear out nowadays. Most TV ads are only seen a handful of times. Prompted ad awareness scores are typically well under 40%. And even when TV weights were higher, there was little evidence of good campaigns wearing out. A major manufacturer once reviewed thousands of econometric analyses and concluded that there was no evidence of wear-out in any of their campaigns they'd run anywhere in the world. Our own econometrics tell the same story.

A wonderful example comes from Knorr Stock Cubes. In the 1980s and 1990s, Knorr ran separate advertising in Scotland, extolling the virtues of their stock cubes for home-made soups. This went down well there, because making soup was still central to family life. With no budget for new advertising in this small region, Knorr ran the same ad for ham stock cubes for nearly 10 years. Because Scottish airtime was cheap, the average Scottish housewife (we use that term deliberately) saw that one ad at least 100 times. Yet they still loved it. It became part of folklore. And its catchphrase 'Pea and ham? From a chicken?' passed into the vernacular. Why are we surprised? We all have favourite comedy sketches we know word for word, and still adore.

This 'wear-out myth' is costly. It means unnecessary spending on production, research, agency fees etc. There's another important cost too. Sharp, Ehrenberg and others suggest that marketing works best when it goes with the grain of existing memory structures. Behavioural economics shows, all else being equal, people prefer, and choose, the familiar. Familiarity and consistency boost effectiveness.

If all this is true, we'd expect 'wear-in'. And this does happen. We saw it ourselves years ago, when Barclaycard replaced long-running celebrity spokesman Alan Whicker with Rowan Atkinson in its TV campaign. When Atkinson was introduced, the Awareness Index score 'collapsed' from around nine to around three. It looked like the new ads were performing badly. But to their credit, Barclaycard stuck with them. And three bursts later, the very same ads were scoring 12. The campaign clearly 'wore in' over time.

So there's a genuine dilemma here. On the one hand, ditching ads on spurious wear-out grounds can lead to constant change and reduced effectiveness. On the other hand, powerful new ideas may look weak when initially tested against established campaigns, as the Barclaycard story shows. So ditching and replacing an established campaign is genuinely costly. Sometimes, it's the right thing to do. But often it's not. Pre-testing may not be helpful here. This is one of many situations where judgement is needed – the kind of judgement that requires real marketing skill. Luckily, this is something that wears in over the course of a marketing career.

THE VALUE OF CONSISTENCY
FELIX VS WHISKAS

Useful case study

Back in the 1980s, Whiskas dominated the UK cat food market with over 50% market share.

Felix, on the other hand, was a small, struggling brand that had never been supported. Low in price, and number 6 in market share, it was threatened with de-listing by retailers keen to promote Own Label.

In 1989, Felix's owners had one last roll of the dice. They relaunched the brand in new packaging featuring a black and white cat, who also appeared in their first-ever ad campaign.

Sales increased immediately. So Felix's owners increased investment. Sales increased every year, and Felix became the second fastest growing grocery brand in Britain. Price elasticity fell too, allowing Felix's owner to raise prices. Soon, Felix had repositioned itself as a premium brand.

The campaign evolved over time, but the black and white cat was consistently used. Felix appeared in press, on TV and posters. He appeared on tea towels, tea pots and advent calendars. Soon he was being used consistently across Europe.

Whiskas, on the other hand, followed the fashionable theory of 'disruption'. Each creative execution was completely new, with no consistency. The thinking being that this would make Whiskas more interesting than its rival – still using the same black and white cat for nearly 30 years.

But Whiskas' strategy was disastrous. Market share tumbled. Felix overtook Whiskas in its core territory, despite much smaller budgets.

Felix's success seemed baffling to many marketers. Unlike Whiskas, Felix ads contained few product messages. And, unlike Whiskas, the same Felix executions ran for years, with few changes.

But Felix's advertising was much more efficient than Whiskas', because it was more consistent. By constantly reinforcing the association between Felix and the amusing antics of their cute cartoon cat, Felix brand preference was strengthened, leading to long-term sales growth, increased distribution, reduced price sensitivity and increased margins. As a result, efficiency and ROI steadily increased over time.

Marketers fret about wear-out. But this Felix case shows that great advertising often becomes *more* effective over time. In mature markets at least, consistency can be more profitable than 'disruption'.

CONSISTENCY VS CHANGE

2 minute checklist

o   Don't fall for the 'disruption' schtick. In marketing, consistency is usually better.

o   Remember: we mostly buy on autopilot, guided by associations formed over many years. Think of these associations in our minds as like a well-trodden path through a grassy field.

o   Mess with these associations at your peril. They keep people buying your brand.

o   Take a lesson from the world of pack design. There, owned associations are managed in a rigorous, consistent way. Change is less frequent. When it does occur, it's evolutionary. Disruptive change is rare.

o   Don't be cavalier about owned associations in the world of advertising. They're slow and expensive to build, but easy to chuck away.

o   Think in terms of campaigns, not executions. Don't routinely junk old ads for new ones. Don't change campaigns before necessary. Don't dismiss slogans and jingles as 'old school'.

o   Don't be overly concerned about wear-out. Millward Brown concludes that genuine wear-out is rare, and limited to 'new news' ads. Campaigns are more likely to wear *in* than out.

o   If your ads do seem to be wearing out, try
    changing your media strategy. What looks like
    wear-out is often just excessive frequency.

o   Worry more about wear-in. Remember: brand associations
    are built through repetition.

o   Be strategic about managing continuity and change.

o   Be rigorous in coding brand memory structures: colour, sound,
    end-line, logo, mnemonic etc. Write them into your 'brand key' or
    whatever you use. Police your memory structures. Use them
    consistently and ruthlessly across everything you do.

o   Consistency should be your default. Not change.

o   When a campaign does need to change, work out the 'footsteps
    through your campaigns'. Balance familiarity with freshness. What can
    you keep from your current campaign to build on existing memory
    associations?

THE POWER OF BRAND MEMORY STRUCTURES

THE LLOYDS BLACK HORSE

Useful case study

Cropping up again and again in our checklists you'll notice mention of 'brand memory structures'. What music, colour, logo, slogan, character etc is effortlessly linked in people's minds to your brand? Do you have any memory structures? Have you written them into your 'brand onion'? Do you rigorously police their usage? Do you use them consistently? Have you set out to create them if you don't have anything? Can you resurrect an association you used to have, but have somehow lost along the way?

Ease of brand linkage to the ideas we create is one of the easiest things to misjudge or overlook. We've all done it. Because when we work so closely with our brand, its link to what we produce is bleedin' obvious to us. We forget, though, to make it easy for a disinterested, busy, low-attention real person to connect our comms with our brand. Data from Ehrenberg-Bass suggests that the majority of all ads are either ignored, or if they are noticed, people have no idea what brand the ad is for. That's the majority of ads essentially wasting money.

The good news is that many brands have powerful links with some sort of memory structure, even if they're no longer used. These links last years, often decades, in our minds. So they can be resurrected, dusted off and refreshed to great commercial effect. The Lloyds Black Horse is a great example of this. Lloyds' 250 years anniversary campaign in 2015 put the heroic Black Horse back at the heart of an emotionally powerful campaign idea. And it paid huge dividends. Latent associations between Lloyds and the horse were turbocharged. As a result, efficiency (and effectiveness) campaign measures stunningly increased.

	Correct Brand Attribution	Branded Recall	Efficiency
(all indexed vs benchmark =100)			
Campaign before reintroduced Black Horse campaign	84	113	128
New Black Horse campaign 2015	185	206	286

Base: Lloyds non customers

* efficiency = combined measure of branding/distinctiveness relative to spend

CREATIVITY AND EFFECTIVENESS DO NOT GO TOGETHER

'The most effective ads don't sell, but they do make people buy'
Ian Leslie

'That Samsung ostrich ad? – funny, but don't suppose it sold many phones'. 'Ah, but Cadbury's "Gorilla" ad didn't actually work, did it?' 'Those John Lewis Christmas ads make me cry. But will they make me buy anything there?'

We've all heard these questions whenever ground-breaking comms emerge. Yes, it's funny. Or beautifully shot. Or tear-jerking. But will it actually sell anything? There seems to be an implicit assumption among many marketing people that creativity and effectiveness are awkward bedfellows. Creative ads bring fame and awards. But the ads that really sell stuff are much more workmanlike.

So it's fascinating when research busts

this most hardwired of marketing myths. Peter Field has analysed the relationship between creativity and effectiveness. Using the IPA's Databank, he took a huge number of campaigns, comparing performance in creative awards around the world with business results.

So does the creativity needed to win major creative awards improve a brand's chance of business success?

The answer? An emphatic 'yes'. Ads that win creative awards are much more effective than ads that don't. And the more creative awards they win, the more effective they tend to be. But the most striking finding is how *efficient* creative campaigns are. Ads that win creative awards are 11 times more efficient at selling stuff than other ads. That's an astonishing finding. It suggests creativity is almost certainly the most important tool at the marketing director's disposal.

The research also highlights two reasons *why* award-winning ads work so well. The first is obvious. Highly creative campaigns get people talking, on and offline, about the brand and the advertising. This amplifies direct effects of the campaign. The second reason is more controversial. Ads that win creative awards tend to be high on emotional impact and lower than average on rational content.

Conventional marketing wisdom says that to shift product you need to get your selling message across. But conventional wisdom is wrong. Emotions have more influence over people's buying behaviour than rational product messages. John Lewis Christmas TV ads say nothing rational about what John Lewis sells. But their ROI grows every year – currently over £10 for every pound spent. Highly creative *and* highly successful.

So why is this myth that creative ads don't work so pervasive? Some clients seem uncomfortable with the very idea that ads without messages could work. Because if these ads do move sales, that's a challenge to their models of communication. Surely their company can't have been wrong all these years in their systems and benchmarks?

Research evidence is building which shows that this emotional selling approach, so prevalent in award-winning ads, doesn't tend to perform well in conventional quantitative pre-testing. How many potentially business-changing campaigns are piling up in that animatic graveyard?

This leaves us with an intriguing and counterintuitive thought: those 'creative types' judging on creative awards panels, for all their oft-maligned focus on the ground-breaking and provocative, may actually turn out to be more skilled at predicting an ad's business success than the thousands of dollars routinely invested in pre-testing systems…

Economist John Maynard Keynes once said: 'There is nothing so disastrous as a rational investment policy in an irrational world'. He would need to look no further than a lot of current pre-testing for proof he was right.

PRE-TESTING AND EMOTIONAL ADVERTISING

2 minute checklist

o   Understand that most pre-testing is still grounded in older, 'System 2' models of how advertising works.

o   If you do pre-test, look for systems that take account of 'System 1' effects too.

o   Help clients understand that they don't need to do well on *all* measures. Emotional brand ads don't need to score well on 'persuasion'; rational activation doesn't need high 'affinity'.

o   Identify and agree with your clients which pre-test 'scores' are important for *this* ad and *this* task. Do this before the scores arrive.

o   Focus on the 'bookends' of the ad development process. Do upfront qualitative research to get your strategy right. Then do sales analysis to learn what *actually* works in the marketplace.

o   Spend less time on the 'middle' of the process: pre-testing propositions and animatics. Be more like John Lewis: prefer econometric post-testing to pre-testing.

o   Be realistic if you are going to pre-test. Accept that no pre-test is 100% accurate. It's hard enough to evaluate effectiveness in retrospect. Let alone predict it.

o   Accept that you'll always need to use judgement and experience. If you're not able or willing to do this, you're not up to your job.

o   Don't go 'blind' into quantitative research.
    Do qualitative research first. It's not infallible, but
    it helps enormously. You get a holistic view of how
    individual people react to the ad as a whole vs responses
    to individual questions.

o   Pre-test finished films if possible. If not, spend time and money
    on getting a great rough version.

o   Be aware of what can't be captured in an animatic – a comedic look?
    Amazing-looking food? Unconventional beauty?

o   Remember: identical ads with different music pre-test differently. Test
    with the music track you'll actually use.

o   Always get the questionnaire and go through it in detail. Ask yourself how
    you'd answer the question. Check wording. Check translations. Check the
    sample. Remember: people who're not in the market for your specific
    product may react differently from people who are.

o   Add questions relating specifically to your ad if you can. Remove
    redundant questions. Long questionnaires are bad questionnaires.

o   If possible, analyse responses by sub-sample. Sometimes this gives
    more confidence in results than a wider sample score.

o   Consider trying new, 'System 1' approaches to research – from
    simple questions about feelings to implicit attitude testing or
    neuroscience.

Notes:

_____

_____

_____

_____

_____

_____

_____

_____

EFFECTIVENESS AND EVALUATION

'Be creative and measure what happens. If it works, do more of it. If it doesn't work, go back and be creative again'

Leslie Moeller and Edward Landry

NINE

INTRODUCTION

Our final chapter looks at effectiveness: how to define, measure and improve it.

We start with the distinction between effectiveness and efficiency. These are closely related, but can point in opposite directions, especially in marketing. We explain why effectiveness matters more. And why focusing on efficiency can be disastrous.

Next, how to improve effectiveness by making marketing more accountable. There's a lot of talk about 'accountability' and 'effectiveness', but we often make accountability difficult and effectiveness less likely. Our second article shows how to get it right.

Part of the answer is to measure the right things. Too often the tail wags the dog. Marketers focus on things they can measure easily. Not what's important. The third article shows which metrics to pay most attention to.

Having the right data isn't enough, though. Simplistic analysis means misleading conclusions. Our fourth article looks at

the 'Rosser Reeves fallacy' – a flawed evaluation approach still alive and well despite being discredited 60 years ago. We show how to evaluate activity properly.

The next three articles look at online evaluation. Digital data is great, but it doesn't solve all evaluation problems. A lot of online analysis is simplistic and misleading. More sophisticated 'attribution models' and testing systems are emerging, but won't be complete until they measure longer term interactions between online and offline worlds. Until then, 'real-time evaluation' may make marketing *less* effective.

Next, risk. Advertising is unpredictable, so 'risky' in a sense. But it's actually hard to go disastrously wrong. Far more risky to spend ages getting it 'just right'. We show how to manage risk without stifling creativity, and turn failure to your advantage.

Finally, we discuss advertising – art or science?

YOU CAN ~~NEVER~~ BE TOO EFFICIENT

'It's no use sharpening the bit if you're drilling in the wrong place'
John Paul Getty

We had an email exchange with a client the other day. It was about measuring the profitability of a campaign. It seemed we were talking at cross-purposes. Until we realised why. We thought we were talking about profit. But they were talking about ROI. And they thought it meant the same thing.

This happens a lot these days. In much the same way that 'brand equity' was used a decade or so ago, there's a perception that 'ROI' is a good thing, without much appreciation of what it means. People talk as if profit and ROI were interchangeable. But they're not. And it's important to understand the difference.

Suppose you spend £10 million on a campaign, and the profit on extra sales generated is £11 million. Then net profit, after subtracting the campaign cost, is

£1 million. Net profit is a good measure of effectiveness – the more profit, the more effective the campaign.

ROI, on the other hand, is a measure of efficiency, not effectiveness. It's calculated by taking the ratio of net profit generated (£1 million) to the cost of the campaign (£10 million). In this case, ROI is 10%.

ROI can be a useful measure – for comparing different ways of spending budget, for example. But making ROI your primary focus can be dangerous. To understand why, you need to think about diminishing returns.

As you spend more on advertising, it often gets more effective (sales and profits generated go up), but less efficient (ROI goes down). That's the nature of diminishing returns. It means that in practice the highest ROIs tend to come from small budgets. Compare our previous example with a small budget campaign (see table below). If your aim was to maximise ROI, you'd go for the small budget campaign. But that would mean smaller profit. Going for the big budget campaign would mean lower ROI, but bigger profit.

And that's the nub of it. As Tim Ambler points out in his classic article 'ROI is dead: now bury it', advertisers should try to maximise profits, not ROI. ROI is usually highest when sales and budget are close to zero. So trying to maximise ROI is a good way to destroy your brand.

This confusion is one example of a general confusion between effectiveness and efficiency. They're often used interchangeably, but can point in different directions. Effectiveness is about reaching targets. So, sales and profit are effectiveness measures. Efficiency is about how much effort you expend to achieve a given effect. ROI is an efficiency measure.

Sometimes, effectiveness and efficiency go hand in hand. In manufacturing, broadening the market for your product is often effective (sales and profit go up) *and* efficient (unit costs go down and margins go up). But in comms, they tend to be opposites. IPA research shows that, while pure direct response activity is a highly efficient way to spend budgets, it's not very effective on its own. Sales effects tend to be small and short term (as Heinz found to its cost in the 1990s, when it briefly junked all advertising in favour of DM).

Long-running brand campaigns, however, tend to be highly effective (big sales and profit effects), but less efficient without the support of activation channels like DM and search.

Ideally, we should be effective *and* efficient. IPA research suggests that this means spending the majority of budget on brand (effective), supported by lower spend on direct (efficient). But effectiveness matters most. Better to achieve your goals inefficiently than be a gloriously efficient failure.

	Adspend	Net Profit	ROI
Big budget campaign	£10,000,000	£1,000,000	10%
Small budget campaign	£100,000	£50,000	50%

EFFECTIVENESS AND EFFICIENCY

2 minute checklist

o Understand the difference between effectiveness and efficiency. They're not the same.

o Make effectiveness (the extent to which you achieve your goals) your primary concern.

o Treat efficiency (ratio of effectiveness to effort) as a secondary consideration.

o Never make efficiency your sole focus. That leads to budget cuts, falling sales and shrinking profits.

o Concentrate on effectiveness. Aim to maximise profit (financial effectiveness), not ROI (financial efficiency).

o Set clear objectives. If you don't, you're bound to fail (see Chapter 1 for more detail).

o Start with business objectives. How will this make a profit? How much do you need to sell? At what price?

o Then set marketing objectives. Who do you need to talk to? What do you want them to do?

o Finally, think about communications objectives. How many people do you need to reach? What do you want them to think and feel? How will communications achieve that?

o   Get the timing right. Better to get it roughly
    right now than waste a year making it perfect.
o   Allocate enough budget. The best campaign in the
    world will fail without investment.
o   Set and allocate budget to maximise effectiveness first,
    efficiency second.
o   Lead with brand-building activity – it's the most effective tool in
    your armoury.
o   Support this with high-performance activation – it increases efficiency.
o   Balance the two by splitting your budget roughly 60% brand, 40%
    activation.
o   Improve efficiency where you can. But make sure you're comparing
    like with like. Be wary about shifting budget between brand and
    activation. They do different jobs over different timescales.
o   Don't get too excited about small-scale activities that seem highly
    efficient. Those efficiencies will probably disappear if you spend
    more on them.

HOW ~~NOT~~ TO IMPROVE EFFECTIVENESS

'Any metric which becomes a target, loses its value as a metric'
'Goodhart's law'

A client recently briefed us on an evaluation project. As they outlined the questions they wanted answers to, a feeling of déjà vu crept over us.

We'd worked on this brand for years. A quick look through our files showed all these questions had been already answered by previous research. But clearly it was easier to keep asking the same questions than learning from and acting on the answers.

Clients and agency people talk a lot about 'accountability' and 'effectiveness'. But actually, both sides behave in ways that make accountability difficult and effectiveness less likely.

Let's start with the briefing process. Common sense, and now empirical evidence, tells us that the clearer a campaign's objectives, the more likely it is to succeed. Setting hard targets for behavioural change and business results are particularly important.

Yet many briefs are still vague about what communications are expected to do. Objectives, if set at all, are usually based on intermediate measures (awareness or response rates), not measures like sales or profit. Precise, timed targets are rarer still.

And there's a similar lack of rigour when it comes to evaluation. Performance metrics are chosen on easy-to-measure criteria. Not on importance for long-term brand health.

So advertising continues to be assessed in terms of ad awareness (even though the link with sales and profit is often tenuous) because it's a simple metric. Direct response rates are popular barometers of effectiveness, even though they're short-term effects, don't necessarily represent incremental business, and are driven by factors besides marketing. Online activity is assessed by online responses – easy to measure, but evidence shows real payback takes place offline for most brands. Direct response activity is favoured over brand building, because direct responses are easy to count. Rational communication is preferred to emotional approaches, because it's easier to ask someone if they remember a proposition than to measure the warmth they feel towards your brand.

Poorly thought-out business incentives can be dangerous. We had one client whose annual bonus was based entirely on one advertising pre-test score. Not surprisingly, his focus was on this score, regardless of wider business effects (an example of what Charles Channon, instigator of the IPA Effectiveness Awards, called 'Organisational Validity': evaluation according to what's good enough internally to justify your decision). Even when good evaluation systems are in place, there's a tendency to use them to confirm existing beliefs. So billions are poured into trying to grow brands by increasing loyalty, even though years ago Ehrenberg showed it's more or less impossible.

But the biggest problem is probably failure to learn. Our research client was a particularly bad example – they had all the answers needed, but weren't interested in them. Most companies have problems like this. Data gets lost. Research reports are forgotten. Personnel come and go. It's hardly surprising companies seem incapable of learning from their mistakes.

We read an interesting article about the rise of data analytics to guide the transfer fees of professional footballers. Football used measures like numbers of tackles per match to assess players, because this was readily available data. But by the mid-2000s, it became clear that these numbers had no correlation with match outcomes. Subsequent analysis discovered the numbers that did differentiate players and correlate with match results. So clubs changed their evaluation approach to measure and value new things like 'high-intensity output' (players' ability to make repeated sprints).

If only our industry was similarly open to new learning when it comes to evaluation and effectiveness.

ACCOUNTABILITY AND EFFECTIVENESS

2 minute checklist

o   Remember: effectiveness (doing the right thing) is more important than accountability (being *seen* to do the right thing).

o   Effectiveness starts with the brief. Set clear objectives and spell out how to achieve them.

o   Think about evaluation from the start. Choose KPIs to measure effectiveness at each stage. Let your plan determine your metrics. Not vice versa.

o   Measure the right things. If your aim is first-time trial, then measure actual trial, not penetration.

o   Allocate time and money for measurement and analysis. Make sure samples are big enough to measure the effects you expect. Consider building tests into your plan.

o   Beware focusing on a single number. Create a 'Balanced Scorecard', with several KPIs (not too many). Set targets for each KPI.

o   Set business targets first. Prioritise long-term profit over short-term sales. Value over volume. And relative performance over absolute numbers.

o   Then set behavioural targets. Prioritise long-term buying behaviour over short-term response. And penetration over loyalty.

o   Then set attitudinal targets. Brands' metrics often
    move together, so consider targeting a 'metric of metrics'
    or brand equity score. Remember that these usually lag
    behavioural change.

o   Finally, measure media exposure in terms of reach, frequency,
    cost per thousand etc.

o   Now look at how brands like yours usually behave. Are your
    targets and budgets realistic?

o   Take care with Performance-Related Pay (PRP). It can improve
    effectiveness, or destroy it. The devil is in the detail.

o   For PRP, targets should be quantitative, with timings and budgets
    attached.

o   If you change plan or budget, revise targets accordingly.

o   Think carefully about incentives – they can distort behaviour and screw
    everything up.

o   Beware schemes that encourage people to focus on a single number.
    Prefer a more rounded assessment of performance.

o   Keep PRP bonuses modest, and retain an element of judgement,
    or people will try to 'game the system'.

HOW ~~NOT~~ TO MEASURE EFFECTIVENESS

'Not everything that can be counted counts, and not everything that counts can be counted'
William Bruce Cameron

Recently, we've been helping some clients assess their latest ad campaign. It's a great little campaign and seems to have boosted sales and market share. But evaluation is complicated because of the number of media used. Most of the budget was spent on traditional media, particularly TV and Outdoor. The remainder was spent on a mix of digital channels, mobile messaging and PR stunts. Working out the contribution of each is hard.

At the first meeting, our clients presented a detailed review of each media used. And something struck us as odd. Traditional media, which accounted for almost three quarters of the budget, were dismissed in about

15 minutes. Then nearly two hours was devoted to the smaller, newer media. In fact, it seemed the less money spent on a channel, the more attention it got.

One reason was that there was simply more data on the newer, digital channels. Slide after slide was presented, packed with figures on number of views, clicks, likes, shares, tweets, followers, comments and uploads. Dwell times and conversion metrics were analysed in forensic detail. But for TV, only one number was presented: the cost. This is a clear example of data tail wagging evaluation dog. Don't focus on what's important (ie the media where most money was at stake), focus on what's easy to measure.

The other problem with this baffling array of metrics is that it's impossible to compare like with like. How do you compare tweets with likes? How do these relate to click-through rates? In the absence of a 'common currency', there's no way to assess relative performance, other than through sheer volume of data. So it would be easy to come away from that meeting with the impression that digital and mobile channels were the main sales drivers. And traditional media were just a sunk cost.

However, some weeks later we saw another analysis which gave a different picture.

Instead of getting lost in all the different metrics available for each channel, this new analysis simplified things. Through lots of digging, the analysts managed to work out total impressions achieved for each campaign element. These were then combined with spend figures to calculate cost per impression. That simplified things hugely. Although, paradoxically, it required a lot more work, as these metrics weren't routinely reported in this comparable way.

The results of this comparative analysis were a bit of an eye-opener. Suddenly the traditional poster elements of the campaign were revealed as delivering the greatest number of impressions in a very cost-effective way. Meanwhile, the newer elements of the campaign, like geo-targeted mobile comms, delivered tiny levels of reach at eye-watering cost.

Exposure analysis is no substitute for full econometric modelling. But it's a pretty good place to start, and very revealing. Did you know that YouTube can be twice as expensive as TV? Or advertising on London bus-sides for one week can deliver more impressions than a 3-month Twitter campaign? Or mobile messaging is 120 times more expensive than Facebook advertising? Our clients didn't. Neither did we.

The learning here is that, unless you take time to compare apples with apples, true comparative analysis is impossible, and dangerously subjective elements creep in. Don't allow a desire to do the cool new stuff blur the true picture of the media fruit bowl.

EVALUATION METRICS

2 minute checklist

o Choose metrics carefully. They influence
   decision making, especially if bonuses are at stake.

o Choose metrics that reflect your strategy. Not the data
   you happen to have.

o Think about how your campaign will work. Outline a clear
   causal chain from communications to behaviour to profit.
   Measure performance for each link in the chain.

o Focus on how your campaign works in the real world. If you pre-test,
   choose finished films over animatics. And in-market tests not the lab.

o Measure exposure for all channels – it's the main determinant of media
   effectiveness. Compare exposure by channel, on a like-for-like basis.

o Correct digital data for degree of exposure (percentage of ad on screen)
   and dwell time. Exclude non-humans and other viewers outside your
   target market.

o Pay more attention to reach than cost per thousand. If you pour money
   into cheap media, you may just end up hitting the same people again
   and again.

o Experiment with new media on a small scale, to see what works.
   But devote most attention to your big media investments. It's
   important to get them right.

o   Measure the *response* to exposure, in terms
    of attitudes (brand ads), direct responses (activation)
    and sales. It's not enough to know you got a thousand
    mentions or 100,000 views.

o   Tailor your metrics to the way your activity works. Message
    -driven ads should be evaluated differently from emotional ads,
    promotions and direct response differently from long-term
    brand building. Beware a one-size-fits-all approach.

o   Use tracking for diagnosis. Not for evaluation. Ads can get sales
    without awareness, and vice versa.

o   Pay more attention to actual behaviour than questionnaire responses.
    Pay more attention to long-term behavioural metrics (eg penetration)
    than short-term ones (eg clicks).

o   Make business results your ultimate measure of effectiveness. Focus on
    market share more than raw sales, value more than volume, and profit
    more than revenue. Look for 'longer and broader' effects like
    reductions in price sensitivity or increases in distribution.

o   Take account of all the other factors that influence sales: price,
    distribution, seasonality etc.

o   Use econometrics, attribution modelling or some form of testing
    to measure the *incremental* sales and profit generated.

HOW ~~NOT~~ TO PROVE THAT ADVERTISING WORKS

'Why, sometimes I've believed as many as six impossible things
before breakfast'
The Queen, 'Alice in Wonderland' (Lewis Carroll)

Recently, a planner came to us with exciting research findings. She was trying to evaluate the effect of a new campaign, and had found a great bit of evidence. A research company had shown that people who recognised the ad had a much better image of the brand, and were significantly more likely to buy it. Perfect proof that it worked, surely?

No. This particular mistake has been going strong for over 50 years. It's even got a name: the 'Rosser Reeves fallacy'. And it's still alive and kicking today.

Rosser Reeves, in his 1961 book *Reality in Advertising*, outlined a simple method for measuring ad effectiveness. Take a sample of your target audience. Ask them about your brand. Then show them your ad and see how many recognise it. Compare brand scores for ad recognisers with brand scores for non-recognisers. Hey presto, there's your ad effect!

Reeves' method is quick, simple and nearly always shows big ad effects. It's also completely flawed. The problem is that people are more likely to notice and remember ads for brands they know well and like. So usually ad recognition is the effect. Not the cause.

You must have noticed this yourself. You buy a new car. Suddenly you see ads for it everywhere. You start working on a brand. And suddenly you spot it everywhere. Familiarity with a brand primes us to notice and remember its advertising. So even if you exclude brand users, you'll always see a spurious correlation between brand and ad responses.

Reeves' methodology was discredited decades ago. But as our planner found, research companies continue to peddle it, and clients and agencies continue to be seduced by it. And now it seems to be mutating into a new, dangerous strain.

Some years ago, a research project looking into the effects of online marketing for FMCG brands was published (see later in chapter). Using a panel of a million internet users, it proved conclusively that people who visit a brand's website are more likely to buy that brand and spend more on it than other buyers.

But this is just another new incarnation of the Rosser Reeves problem: correlation is not proof of causation. In fact, closer examination of the data reveals that people who visit a brand's website tend to spend a lot on the *category*. They're actually less loyal to the brand, and tend to pay less for it per purchase. This suggests they're deal hunters – probably what brings them to the website.

Similarly, we often come across research supposedly 'proving' the effectiveness of social media by showing a brand's Facebook fans tend to be heavier buyers. Yes, they are. That's why they become fans.

These new digital incarnations of the 'Rosser Reeves fallacy' are dangerous. Because they focus on heavy buyers they lead to flawed emphasis on loyalty over penetration, targeting over reach, and price promotion over brand building – all strategies proven to be less profitable.

The right way to deal with these spurious correlations is through controlled exposure. Take two identical groups of people. Expose one lot to your advertising and leave the other group unexposed. Then compare attitudes and behaviour between the two groups over the course of the test. These 'controlled exposure tests' take more time, effort and money. But they produce more accurate and sensible results – showing advertising does work, but not always, and revealing that short-term ad effects are modest, but still worthwhile. When applied to digital activity, they seem to produce similarly realistic findings.

This is the true 'reality in advertising'. Perhaps someone should write another book?

EVALUATION METHODS

2 minute checklist

o   Don't rely too much on 'soft' questionnaire
    data. Even when people are honest, they forget the
    things they do, and have a poor understanding of why
    they do them.

o   Watch out for spurious correlations between tracking metrics
    (eg the 'Rosser Reeves effect'). Test for causality. Separate users
    from non-users – if your correlations disappear, they're probably
    bogus. Look at trends over time – do effects follow causes?

o   Remember: tracking metrics don't actually measure effectiveness.
    Ads can be highly effective without shifting tracking scores much.

o   So use 'hard' data where you can. Measure actual (not claimed)
    behaviour and business results. Compare them against actual campaign
    exposure. Not claimed recall or recognition.

o   Use 'soft' data to understand *how* (not whether) your campaign works.

o   Simply counting direct responses isn't enough. That attributes every
    response or sale to the last touchpoint. This is just wrong.

o   Try more sophisticated 'attribution modelling' to analyse direct
    responses (which claim to solve the 'last click attribution' problem
    – see more on this in the next article). This is a
    specialised area; get an expert to help.

o   Or use econometrics. This gives a better
    reading of overall effectiveness, especially for
    brand-building activity.

o   Build tests into your plan if you can. Divide your audience
    into different groups. Expose them to different things. See
    how they respond.

o   Test at the individual or regional level ('geo testing'). Test different
    copy (A/B tests) and different levels of exposure. Test different
    combinations of channels.

o   Run tests over long periods, if you want to pick up long-term effects.
    The very best tests have run for several years.

o   Use all this information in your models. Build models with data at the
    regional or individual level ('single source data') if you have it.

o   But be aware that there's no single, fool-proof way of measuring
    effectiveness. All techniques have limitations. Use multiple
    metrics and methods.

HOW NOT TO EVALUATE DIGITAL ACTIVITY

Useful insight

Over the last 20 years or so, clients have spent huge sums of money building websites where people can engage with their brands. For some, the benefits have been obvious. But for FMCG brands, which don't usually sell direct online, the payback is less clear.

So there was great excitement back in 2012 when a major study was published, claiming to measure the effect of having a web presence on packaged goods sales. Based on a panel of 1 million internet users, the research looked at correlations between browsing behaviour and consumption of 10 packaged goods brands. And the results looked dramatic. According to the report, people who visited a brand's website were '48% more likely to buy the brand' and spent 37% more than other people.

At the time, this was hailed as a breakthrough in digital evaluation. But let's take a closer look.

You might expect people who visit a brand's website to be real fans. But crunch the numbers, and you reach the opposite conclusion. People who visit a brand's website are *less* loyal and *more* likely to buy competing brands. And they tend to *pay less* for the product, both in absolute terms and relative to rival brands.

But if these people aren't fans, why go to the website? The clue is that these people tend to be heavy buyers of the category, spending 53% more on it than non-visitors. Now if you spend a lot of money on detergent (say), it may be worth your

Visitors to a brand's website are 48% more likely to buy

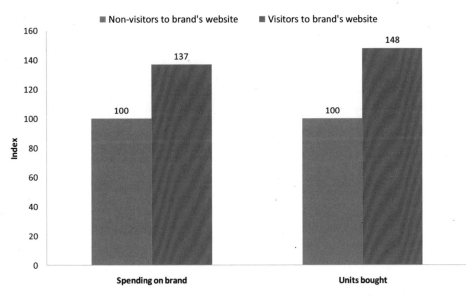

Source: 'Are Your CPG brands maximizing the return on your digital investment?' Accenture, Comscore, Dunnhumby, 2012

Sample: Integrated Comscore/Dunnhumby panel of 1 million internet users, 10 FMCG brand websites, September 2010–February 2011

while to shop around for special offers, and brand websites often feature them. This may explain why web visitors are less brand loyal (they shop around more), and tend to pay less (they tend to buy stuff on special offer).

So yes, web visits do *correlate* with purchases. But that doesn't mean that visiting a website *makes people buy*. It's just as likely that people visit *because they're about to buy*. And if that's true, then the true sales effect will be much smaller than this report suggested. Indeed, if brands are offering generous discounts online, then the financial effects might even be negative.

This kind of simplistic analysis is all too common in the digital world. So next time someone tells you that some online behaviour correlates with sales, remember: correlation is not causation.

ONLINE, EVALUATION IS ~~NO LONGER~~ A PROBLEM

'It is better to be vaguely right than exactly wrong'
Carveth Read

Listen to any speech at any marketing conference these days, and before long the brave new world of 'evaluation in the digital age' is celebrated. This new world means no adspend is wasted, uncertainty is eliminated, and we have full accountability, as the evaluation game is raised to hitherto unknown heights.

Dig a bit deeper, and you'll find much of this promise is a false dawn.

Yes, we have more data than ever before. Yes, technologically, online measurement is sophisticated. But analytically, we're not so impressed. A lot of online evaluation is pretty basic. We saw an example recently. A brand with large media spend across many channels analysed response by channel and concluded that conventional advertising did nothing for its business, because all responses came via other channels.

An industry fault is that we tend to see the world in discrete camps: buyer/non-buyer; Generation X/Generation Y; heavy user/light user. Not surprising then that we view online and offline worlds separately. This can lead to dangerously oversimplified conclusions about the effectiveness of digital spend, getting nowhere near measuring true effectiveness. Most digital evaluation is based on the direct response paradigm – really just a variation on the evaluation that mail-order companies did 100 years ago. Run a banner ad. Count the number of responses it gets. Then work out ROI.

But this gets the numbers wrong. Why becomes clear when we put aside discrete boxes and consider digital in a wider context.

First, there's the 'last click attribution' problem. Suppose a thousand people clicked on our banner ad. Simplistic analysis attributes all these clicks to the last click: the banner. But in reality, those clicks will have been partly due to other marketing activity. To measure the contribution of the banner properly, we need to account for these other influences, including offline marketing like TV ads and posters.

Secondly, there's often a cannibalisation issue. Not all those clicks are incremental business. Some responses would have happened anyway without the banner. And some might have happened offline: people phoning a call centre or walking into a shop. To measure the effect of the banner properly, we need to understand how it affects these other channels.

Thirdly, there may be 'halo effects' not being measured this way. Some people who see the banner may go straight to the website, pick up the phone or go into an actual physical shop, rather than clicking through.

All three effects show the importance of understanding the inter-relationships between online and offline worlds.

As an industry, we focus on change at the expense of the unchanging. But contrary to what people think, most life still takes place offline, not online. Recent IPA TouchPoints data shows that more than 80% of all media consumption is offline. And, while social media and online spending are growing strongly, still over 80% of communication and spending happens offline.

So, sophisticated digital evaluation giving true digital ROIs needs to measure how both online and offline media drive sales, both online and offline.

Fortunately, we're beginning to learn how to do this. Analysts are using econometrics to measure these linkages, not relying on simple direct response techniques 100 years out of date.

So with evaluation, the real excitement is not what's happening now. The real digital revolution will occur only when we stop treating 'online' and 'offline' as two discretely different worlds. Then we'll be able to measure its true potential.

ONLINE DATA HAS ~~NO~~ LIMITATIONS

'We are in danger of valuing most highly those things we can measure most accurately'
John Banham, ex-Director General, the CBI

Years ago, when the internet was young, a digital strategist held forth at a meeting: 'The thing about digital marketing,' he said, 'is we know everything about our customers and precisely how they respond to our ads. Online, everything is measurable.'

Back then, evaluating online advertising seemed simple: you counted your click-through rates. And the higher the rate, the more effective the ad. This is a simple and obvious way of measuring effectiveness – one with a long pedigree. It's essentially the same way direct response advertising has been evaluated since the early 1900s. And for all this time, the method has been flawed.

First, it overstates short-term advertising direct effects. Some people who clicked on your banner ad would have come to your website anyway, by another route. Last click attribution is a bit like a retailer attributing sales to each of his shop doors.

The method also ignores longer-term indirect effects. Some people who didn't click on your banner ad will have remembered it, and it may influence purchase later on.

As click-through rates have plummeted, and Google hoovers up much of the last click business, online advertisers now pay more attention to indirect effects. Last click attribution has fallen out of favour, replaced with analysis of the whole online journey.

But this analysis is still fairly basic. Instead of attributing sales to the last click, they're distributed between various 'touchpoints' along the way. It's as if our retailer now admits his sales are driven not just by the doors to his shop but also by the various Tube routes leading to those doors.

This is clearly still nonsense. When we buy something online, it's the result of many encounters with category and brand, often over several years. Even if we're not fully aware of it. The 'customer journey' measurable with short-term cookie data is just the last part of that process.

In fact, online behaviour is largely driven by *offline* influences – hardly surprising, as most of our lives are spent offline. Conversely, a lot of online marketing works by making people buy things offline. Again, not surprising when you realise that more than 80% of retail sales still take place in bricks-and-mortar shops. So any attribution method failing to integrate online and offline data is inevitably flawed.

The old dream that 'everything is measurable online' seems rather hollow now. We now realise it's not always clear how many people actually see the ads we run. Or how many are actually human, let alone in the target audience. And this new scepticism now extends to evaluation. Recently, the CEO of Quantcast said that it's time to expose overly simplistic attribution practices, calling them 'attribution fraud'.

So if online metrics aren't enough on their own – and they're not, because of interactions between offline and online worlds – how should we proceed? Some favour test and control. Take two randomly sampled groups of people but only expose one of them to your online ad. This is essentially the logic behind the traditional regional ad test, although digital technology allows more sophisticated ways of doing it. Both Google and Facebook favour this approach.

The alternative is to build statistical models combining online and offline data. These are often similar to the econometric models offline advertisers have used for years. And they do often show that offline advertising is a big influence on online behaviour.

But these techniques aren't easy to automate. They require skilled researchers with deeper statistical knowledge than most data analysts possess. So, as online marketing matures, it finds itself (paradoxically) reinventing the market research industry it sought to make redundant.

DO ~~NOT~~ LOOK BACK

'History doesn't repeat itself. But it does rhyme'
Mark Twain

As we write, it's IPA Effectiveness Awards season again. For the past few months, agencies have burnt the midnight oil writing papers proving the effectiveness of their campaigns, in great detail. Now the judges will have their summers ruined by having to wade through 60 of these 4,000-word tomes.

We've always taken the awards seriously here at adam&eveDDB. But elsewhere, not everyone is so convinced. 'The IPA Awards?' said a planner from a rival agency recently, 'aren't they past their sell-by date? Real-time evaluation's where it's at now.'

There seems to be growing dissatisfaction with 'traditional' post-campaign evaluation. Critics say it's backward-looking and overly intellectual. What we need is evaluation we can act

on here and now, they say. Hence the brave new world of real-time planning – using 'Big Data' to create 'dashboards' allowing clients and agencies to monitor performance minute by minute, and react accordingly.

Leaving aside the fact that most planners and journalists who're bandying these buzzwords about have no idea what 'Big Data' really means, there's some truth in criticisms of 'old style' evaluation. Too often, it's merely done to win awards or justify budgets; rarely is it used to inform strategy or improve effectiveness.

But there are dangers associated with the real-time approach too. Recent analysis of the IPA Databank shows short-term success metrics are *not* a reliable guide to long-term growth. In fact, focusing on short-term goals can actually reduce clients' long-term profits. The metrics that matter most when it comes to profit simply don't move much in the short term. So they're likely to be ignored when constructing real-time dashboards.

With no longer-term perspective, it becomes hard to monitor and build the long-term, consistent memory structures that are brands. Instead, everything becomes short term, tactical and reactive. Promotions, price cuts and direct-response activity come to the fore because these yield the big, measurable short-term effects. Brand building gets neglected. If we immerse ourselves in the here and now, it becomes harder to learn from the past, and harder to plan for the future. New products and campaigns take time to bed in, and can't easily be evaluated against short-term results.

Building a brand is like flying a plane. You need to monitor your instruments (real-time evaluation). But you also need a map to tell you where you're going and where you've been (long-term evaluation). You need 'Big Data' and 'Long Data'.

Sadly, it seems Big Data is squeezing

Long Data out of the picture. As market research data becomes richer, more detailed and rapidly updated, databases get bigger. And keeping long runs of back data is becoming increasingly costly. With clients and agencies focused on today's numbers, and sceptical about what they learn from the past, research companies are keeping shorter runs of data. If this goes on, we soon won't be able to do long-run analysis at all.

One criticism of the reckless young traders during the 2008 banking crisis was that 'they knew too much maths and not enough history'. Let's hope our industry doesn't go the same way. Perhaps we should take a leaf out of Google Books. Its database allows users to search within texts going back to 1500.

Now that's what we call Long Data.

DIGITAL EVALUATION

2 minute checklist

o   Don't treat online and offline worlds as
     separate siloes: each affects the other.

o   Try to evaluate online and offline activities on a
     like-for-like basis, to allow comparison between them
     (in practice, this is still much harder than it should be).

o   Start by getting reliable and comparable exposure data. Digital
     data needs to improve here. Facebook's announcement that they
     reach 41 million Millennials in the US (when there are in fact only
     31 million of them) is a good example.

o   Don't trust 'last click attribution' methods. They overestimate
     immediate effects of online media, and can't measure effects of offline
     media at all.

o   Prefer more sophisticated attribution models, based on detailed analysis
     of online customer journeys. But be aware they struggle to measure
     anything other than short-term effects, and tend to be 'black boxes'.

o   Note that attribution models struggle to measure the effects of offline
     media, and can't measure offline sales effects at all. Given that more
     than 80% of retail sales still take place offline, this is a huge
     problem for most brands.

o   Use econometric models (with online data)
    to measure these missing effects. Compare or
    combine econometrics with online attribution to give a
    more accurate picture.

o   Watch out for spurious correlations online. For example,
    suppose you target programmatic ads at people who seem
    likely to buy your brand, you'll find that sales correlate with
    exposure, even if the ads don't really work.

o   Use 'controlled exposure tests' to reveal the true effect. At the last
    moment, randomly decide whether people are served your online ad
    or something else. Then compare the behaviour of otherwise similar
    individuals in the 'test' and 'control' groups.

o   Remember: most online data and evaluation is short term, and
    'real-time evaluation' is inherently so. But short-term metrics
    don't predict long-term success. And short-term strategies
    can destroy businesses. Balance Big Data with Long Data.

EFFECTIVENESS IN THE DIGITAL AGE
JOHN LEWIS

Useful case study

If you're looking for a model of how to do effective advertising in the 21st century, forget the 'innovators' and 'disruptors' of Silicon Valley. The best example we know of is a 100-year-old department store based right here in London: John Lewis.

Since 2009, John Lewis has run some of the most effective advertising in Britain, if not the world. Business results have been outstanding, at a time when other retailers have suffered. Paybacks have been enormous. And they've won every effectiveness award going.

How have they done it? The obvious answer: great creative work. John Lewis's highly emotional ads are a hit with the public. And they hoover up creative awards at all the major competitions every year.

But the other essential ingredient has been their media strategy. Unlike some companies, John Lewis bases media schedules on hard empirical evidence, not wishful thinking. All activity is evaluated with econometrics. Then modelling is used to inform the media-planning process.

This gives John Lewis confidence to invest in advertising when many others are cutting back. On average, the store spends around £28 million a year on ad media, according to Nielsen.

About a quarter of that budget is devoted to good old-fashioned TV. Because John Lewis knows TV works. TV gives them huge reach. Over the last four years, TV has yielded a total of 2.5 billion exposures in the UK, more than any digital medium could.

But digital channels make TV work even harder. Online video extends reach even further at zero cost. Paid search converts interest into sales quickly and efficiently.

The result? The most famous advertising in Britain. The launch of the John Lewis Christmas campaign has become an annual ritual. Every year, people rush to see the new ad as soon as it's released. And the press write hundreds of articles about it.

Why not spend less, and adopt a more targeted approach? Because fame makes everything work better. People share the ads with friends. The media give the ads free coverage. And suppliers are increasingly willing to fund them. As a result, every £1 John Lewis spends on advertising generates more than £10 of incremental profit.

John Lewis combines the best of digital and traditional marketing. They have a growing online business. But bricks-and-mortar stores are still the main source of sales. Digital media increase efficiency, but TV is still the biggest driver of growth. Other advertisers take note.

ADVERTISING IS ~~NOT~~ A SAFE INVESTMENT

'It's better to advertise than not advertise. The risk of not acting is much greater than the act of getting it wrong'
Paul Feldwick

Recently we played host to Paul Feldwick, who came into the agency to discuss his latest book. During questions afterwards, a planner asked: 'Failure teaches us more than success, so looking back, which campaign was your biggest failure?'

Paul thought for a bit. Then replied it was actually hard to think of any real disasters. Not because he was infallible, but because it's hard to fail disastrously when it comes to advertising. This struck us as an important thought. Clients often approach advertising with caution. What if the message is wrong? Or our tone of voice isn't right? Or we alienate customers? Or we go against the zeitgeist? Best delay a bit. Do more research. Get it perfect.

As we've written before, however, you'd need to get it spectacularly wrong to generate significant hostility to advertising; the worst that usually happens is indifference. And on the rare occasions when brands do provoke some backlash (eg the recent 'Beach Body Ready' 'uproar' in the UK at Protein World's 'body-shaming poster'), there's always the suspicion that the free publicity generated may actually increase sales. (Understandably, there's little publicly available research on this.)

In over 30 years of evaluation research, we've not seen a single example of an ad campaign that's been shown to have a negative effect on sales. Not one. And it's hard to think of even anecdotal examples. Strand cigarettes? That was more than 50 years ago. And we've never seen empirical evidence that the ad really did harm sales.

One reason it's so hard to fail is what psychologists call the 'mere exposure effect'. Exposing people to any ad for a brand, even just the brand's logo, will increase propensity to choose that brand. No matter what it says. Ads tend to work better if people like them, of course. But even advertising that's disliked can be effective, as the award-winning IPA paper for Radion showed years ago. (A 'hard sell' campaign for a new dirt and odour-removing detergent which was strongly criticised for being harsh and offensive, yet was highly successful in sales terms.)

So most advertising works, to some extent. In all the econometric models we've ever seen, only one TV campaign failed to have a positive sales effect. And that was a single execution with low ratings behind it. (Other media can be harder to measure, but we suspect most of them work just as reliably.)

Of course, increasing sales is not quite enough. A decent campaign should also generate enough cash to pay for itself – and more. Not all manage that, but experienced advertisers can usually avoid making disastrous investments if they follow a few simple rules. Concentrate firepower on markets and brands with big enough sales and decent profit margins (the single biggest factor determining ROI). Choose media that combine low cost per exposure with high emotional power and/or good response rates. Allocate most of your budget to stuff you know delivers a decent ROI, and a bit to testing and learning from new stuff. Piece of cake!

But many clients don't see it like this. They test and tweak in artificial conditions, over-intellectualising and procrastinating. We know one company that spent four years getting their next campaign 'just right', while sales continued to gently decline. They were lucky to get away with it. An analysis we did revealed that two years off air can be enough to kill a brand. Especially if competitors grab this opportunity to ramp up spend and maximise Share of Voice. There's a crowded graveyard of once proud, high-share brands that died from this scenario.

So yes, advertising is unpredictable. It's never possible to know in advance exactly how the public will react to communication until it's out there. And in that sense, it's always risky. But a far bigger risk comes from things we can control – and doing nothing is usually the biggest risk of all.

THERE IS ~~NO~~ VALUE IN FAILURE

'My experience is that we learn much more from failure than
we do from success'
AG Lafley, ex-CEO, P&G

Recently, we found ourselves at the IPA 'Eff Fest': a celebration of all things related to advertising effectiveness. In one session, Paddy Barwise from London Business School showed a collection of social media case studies. The cases were interesting, he said, but they'd be even more interesting if they were about failures. Because we learn so much more from failure than from success.

We agree. And in that spirit, we offer a case study of our own.

Once upon a time, a group of clever agency people had a great new idea for promoting an FMCG brand. It was essentially a price promotion, but delivered in a cool new digital way. The client loved the idea too. Pretty soon,

software developers were hacking through the night to get the thing ready for the brand's peak season.

But just before launch, a kill-joy consultant heard about the project. 'Don't do it,' he said, 'it's going to lose money.' But no-one believed him. And it was too late to stop anyway. The project was indeed a failure. Sales volumes were tiny, and so heavily discounted that they were deeply unprofitable. The client vowed never to do anything like it again.

So, what can we learn from this story?

First, beware fads and fashions. Clever people chose a flawed technological solution, less because it was right, more because it was 'cool'.

Secondly, beware 'groupthink'. Everyone involved in our example loved the new promotional idea. Nobody sought an outside view. The consultant who correctly predicted failure only heard about it by accident.

Thirdly, remember that it's not your money. The team thought about their problem in a very 'Silicon Valley' way: create some cool techy stuff; get it out there quickly; then let the money take care of itself. That may be fine if you're a Google or a start-up with patient investors. But it rightly doesn't play well with established FMCG company boards.

Fourthly, beware hasty decisions. Agencies always have short deadlines. But by the time it was clear this project would fail, it was too late to stop it.

But the biggest lesson of all is to learn from our mistakes. Let's hope that happened in this case. But the project is still trumpeted by many as a great example of creativity.

This tendency to sweep failure under the carpet is pretty universal in our industry. Occasionally, we do get hints of failure. Why did Heinz go back to TV advertising after publicly putting all its money into DM back in the 1990s? Why did Pepsi row back from its decision to make social media the core of its marketing? But public admissions are rare. And case studies non-existent.

Some industries are better at this than we are. Military failures tend to be obvious and public. So do failures of government. As a result, these are two areas where failure's been studied in depth. A 2013 book, *The Blunders of Our Governments*, by Anthony King and Ivor Crewe, categorised factors causing governments to stumble. These included 'groupthink' (a concept arising from the study of the US failure in Vietnam), intellectual fads, hasty decisions and a failure to learn from past mistakes. Our little case study exhibits all of them.

But there *are* some examples from our world of companies brave enough to embrace failure. AG Lafley at P&G introduced a President's 'Fail Forward Award' for teams or individuals that enabled the organisation to 'significantly learn from a failure'.

Maybe it's time for agencies too to start admitting some mistakes. When the IPA holds its inaugural IPA 'Ineff Fest', we'll be in the front row.

MANAGING RISK

2 minute checklist

o   Don't worry, advertising is less risky than it
    seems. *Any* ad increases likelihood to choose the
    brand, regardless of content (the 'mere exposure effect').

o   Don't be afraid that your ads will 'alienate' people. Negative
    effects are rare or non-existent.

o   Worry more about other forms of marketing. Poorly thought-
    out changes to product or packaging can cause sales to plummet.
    Most promotions lose money. And the worst can depress sales for
    months, even years. Bad PR can kill a brand completely.

o   Think about the risk of *not* advertising. Two years without support
    can be enough to send a brand into terminal decline, if competitors
    seize the opportunity.

o   Reduce risk by basing investment decisions on evidence and analysis.
    Not fashionable theories and 'groupthink'. Expose your plan to
    independent scrutiny, preferably by experts.

o   Study your sales and profit figures – these are the biggest
    determinant of marketing ROI. Concentrate your
    firepower on big products and markets with high margins.

o Choose media with low cost per exposure
   and either, a) broad reach and emotional power
   (brand building) or, b) high response rates (activation).

o Allocate most of your budget to stuff that's worked well in
   the past. Continue with old campaigns if they still work. But
   always save a little budget for trying new things. If they work,
   do more.

o Test your ideas on real people early on. Qualitative may be
   more informative than quantitative pre-testing, especially in the early
   stages. Always leave room for judgement and intuition.

o Hone those intuitions by evaluating everything thoroughly. Find out
   what really works, and what doesn't. Keep good records. Learn from
   everything you do. And share this learning.

o Don't be afraid to fail. Failure is a sign of creativity, and it can be a
   wonderful teacher. Limit risks by failing small and fast. When you
   do fail, accept it, acknowledge it, and learn from it.

LEARNING FROM FAILURE
PEPSI REFRESH PROJECT

Useful case study

Back in 2010, Pepsi announced a radical new comms strategy. No more 'mass' Super Bowl ads that cost a fortune to make and air. Instead, their TV budget was going to be switched into a new social media campaign: the 'Pepsi Refresh Project'.

The new idea was for people to nominate social initiatives that would make the world a better place. Other people would vote for the ideas they liked best on social media, and Pepsi would then fund the most popular ones. The Refresh Project wouldn't touch as many Americans as Super Bowl and TV advertising, but the 'engagement' among the people that did see it would more than make up for this. Or so the theory went...

The Refresh Project was a great social media success: millions of Facebook likes and Twitter followers ensued. Trouble was, it didn't sell much Pepsi. The effects were disastrous. In the US, Pepsi and Diet Pepsi both lost around 5% market share in a year. Pepsi dropped to number 3 brand behind Coke and Diet Coke.

The Pepsi Refresh Project quietly fizzled out and Pepsi went back to TV ads. They'd clearly learned some lessons from this. And so can we.

Notes:

_____

_____

_____

_____

_____

_____

_____

_____

A FINAL WORD – ART AND ~~NOT~~ SCIENCE

'The greatest scientists are artists as well'
Albert Einstein

When we signed up to write a monthly column for *Admap* back in 2010, we only committed to doing it for two years. We weren't confident we'd find enough material. Could we really scrape together enough myths and annoyances to fill 22 articles? We needn't have worried. Fast-forward six years, and we'd written over 60, and were still going strong.

Possibly if we'd worked in law, medicine or engineering we'd have found them equally fertile territory. But somehow we doubt it. It seems the world of advertising and marketing is unusually full of frustrating bollocks.

We love this business. But why does it throw up so much, so regularly,

that's so laughably infuriating? We suspect the answer lies in the inherent tension between art and science in our world. A tension that's impossible to resolve. So it fuels an endless supply of frustrations.

On the one hand, a lot of our rants have been about 'unscientific' approaches to marketing. There's no magic formula for effective marketing. But a little due diligence goes a long way. We need to be clear about what we're trying to achieve, and how communication delivers against these goals. We need to understand the market, both qualitatively and quantitatively. What does and doesn't work? Then we need to allocate enough budget to achieve targets.

But too often, this basic spadework is missing. Campaign objectives are either hopelessly vague or laughably unrealistic. (Only recently, a brief demanded the fastest growth in the brand's history with its smallest ever budget.) Plans are made without crunching basic numbers: how many people will this campaign reach? Or are likely to respond? Is that enough to hit our targets? Decades of empirical evidence about how people behave and what makes marketing effective are just ignored.

Then, we cover up this sloppy thinking with language designed to conceal, not reveal, our thinking. Lazy use of words such as 'loyalty' and 'alienation' masks false assumptions about how marketing really works.

On the other hand, lots of our rants have been about overly mechanistic and 'scientific' approaches. Yes, marketing needs planning with informed clarity. But it isn't a science. Human beings are complex. Human communication is subtle. Real people rarely fit into our simplistic targeting and segmentation boxes. They don't pay much attention to our messages. They don't process them deeply. Yet seemingly insignificant things – music, casting, location or a telling detail in the performance – can have huge power. Our work must reflect this; we need magic, not just logic.

Simplistic models of how people respond to marketing are dangerously seductive. Too much evaluation is based on short-term responses or artificial research situations. The result? Marketing that destroys clients' long-term profits. And annoys the public to boot. Simplistic rules never deliver outstanding results, because rule breaking is an inherent part of the creative process.

So over our combined 60 or so years in advertising, we've learnt that it's neither art nor science. It's a bit of both. The tension between the two might be an endless source of frustration. But it's this very tension that makes the job so endlessly fascinating.

USEFUL READING

GENERAL

Barden. P. *Decoded:The science behind why we buy.* Wiley, 2013

Binet, L and Field, P. *Marketing in the Era of Accountability: Identifying the marketing practices and metrics that truly increase profitability.* WARC, 2007

Binet, L and Field, P. *Media in Focus: Marketing effectiveness in the digital era.* IPA, 2017

Binet, L and Field, P. *The Long and the Short of it: Balancing short and long-term marketing strategies.* IPA, 2013

Earls, M. *Herd: How to change mass behaviour by harnessing our true nature.* Wiley, 2009

Feldwick, P. *The Anatomy of Humbug: How to think differently about advertising.* Matador, 2015

Gladwell, M. *Blink: The power of thinking without thinking.* Penguin, 2006

Harari, Y. *Sapiens: A brief history of humankind.* Harper, 2015

Heath, R. *Seducing the Subconscious:The psychology of emotional influence in advertising.* Wiley, 2012

Hoffman, R. *101 Contrarian Ideas about Advertising:The strange world of advertising in 101 delicious bite-size pieces.* Hoffman/Lewis, 2012, and Hoffman's 'Ad Contrarian' blog

Kearon, J, Ewing, T and Wood, O. *System1, Unlocking Profitable Growth.* The System1 Group, 2017

Lehrer, J. *The Decisive Moment: How the brain makes up its mind.* Canongate, 2010

Ritson, M. *Marketing Week* columns

Sharp, B. *How Brands Grow: What marketers don't know.* OUP, 2010

Sharp, B and Romaniuk, J. *How Brands Grow Part 2: Emerging markets, services, durables, new and luxury brands.* OUP, 2015

Shotton, R. *The Choice Factory: 25 behavioural biases that influence what we buy.* Harriman House, 2018

Steel, J. *Truth, Lies and Advertising:The art of account planning.* Wiley, 1998

Thaler, R and Sunstein, C. *Nudge: Improving decisions about health, wealth and happiness.* Penguin, 2009

CHAPTER 1

'Advertising's big questions: answered by advertising's big thinkers'. 'Does advertising grow markets?' Bridget Angear. The Advertising Association, 2016

Binet, L and Field, P. 'Acquisition is the only reliable route to growth'. *Market Leader*, Quarter 2, 2010, WARC

Broadbent, S. 'Does advertising affect market size?' Advertising Association, 1997

Buzzell, R and Gale, B. *The PIMS Principles: Linking strategy to performance.* Macmillan, 1987

Ehrenberg, A. 'My research in marketing'. *Admap*, May 2005, WARC

Kaplan, R and Norton, D. *The Balanced Scorecard: Translating strategy into action.* Harvard Business

Review Press, 1996

Levitt, T. *Marketing Myopia*. Harvard Business Review Classics, 2008

Weigel, M. 'The liberation of magic: how marketing science opens up creative opportunity'. WARC, June 2013

CHAPTER 2

Binet, L. 'The dangers of common sense'. *Market Leader*, Quarter 3, 2009, WARC

Dyson, P. 'Top 10 drivers of advertising profitability'. *Admap*, September 2014, WARC

Dyson, P and Weaver, K. 'Advertising's greatest hits: profitability and brand value'. *Admap*, February 2006, WARC

Graham, C. 'Is your brand's share trying to tell you something?' *Market Leader*, Quarter 1, 2010, WARC

IPA Behavioural Economics Initiative www.IPA. co.uk/BE

Lodish, L and Mela, C. 'If brands are built over years, why are they managed over quarters?' *Harvard Business Review*, July/August 2007

'Pepto-Bismol: from symptoms to occasions'. Effie Silver Award 2012, Effie Worldwide

'Price promotions during the downturn: shrewd or crude?' IPA, June 2009

Pringle, H and Field, P. *Brand Immortality: How brands can live longer and prosper.* Kogan Page, 2008

'What we know about behavioural economics'. WARC Best Practice, 2017

www.ipa.co.uk/Document/Behavioural-Economics-Red-Hot-or-Red-Herring-report

www.ipa.co.uk/Document/Lets-get-practical

www.ipa.co.uk/Document/Were-all-Choice-Architects-now-Second-Edition

CHAPTER 3

Barwise, P and Meehan, S. *Simply Better: Winning and keeping customers by delivering what matters most.* Harvard Business Review Press, 2004

Ehrenberg, A. 'My research in marketing'. *Admap*, May 2005, WARC

Heath, R and Feldwick, P. 'Fifty years using the wrong model of advertising'. *International Journal of Market Research*, January 2008

Hedges, A. *Testing to Destruction: A critical look at the uses of research in advertising*, revised edition. IPA, 1997

Hedges, A. *Testing to Destruction: A fresh and critical look at the uses of research in advertising.* IPA, 1974

CHAPTER 4

Biel, A. 'Love the ad. Buy the product'. *Admap*, September 1990, WARC

Ehrenberg, A. 'The problem of numeracy'. *Admap*, February 1992, WARC

Gordon, W. *Goodthinking: A guide to qualitative research.* NTC Publications, 1999

Gordon, W. *Mindframes: 6 enduring principles from 50 years of market research.* Acacia Avenue, 2016

Harford, T. 'Tim Harford's guide to statistics in a misleading age'. *FT Magazine*, February 2018

CHAPTER 5

Cain, S. *Quiet: The power of introverts in a world that can't stop talking.* Penguin, 2013

Duhigg, C. *The Power of Habit: Why we do what we do, and how to change.* Random House, 2013

Goldacre, B. *Bad Science.* 4th Estate, 2008

Gordon, W. *Mindframes: 6 enduring principles from 50 years of market research.* Chapter 5 'Language beneath the surface of words'. Acacia Avenue, 2016

Leith, S. *You Talkin' to Me? Rhetoric from Aristotle to Obama.* Profile, 2012

Mackay, C. *Extraordinary Popular Delusions and the Madness of Crowds.* Wordsworth Editions, 1995

Slater, N. *Toast: The story of a boy's hunger.* HarperPerennial, 2004

Surowiecki, J. *The Wisdom of Crowds: Why the many are smarter than the few.* Abacus, 2005

www.economist.com/styleguide/introduction

CHAPTER 6

Steel, J. 'Last of the handloom weavers: why planners need to focus on the fundamentals of human nature'. *Admap*, September 2016, WARC

CHAPTER 7

Ambler, T. 'ROI is dead: now bury it'. *Admap*, September 2004, WARC

Binet, L. 'Measuring market payback: a best practice guide'. IPA, 2008 http://adfx.ie/upload/files/1386591541_Measuring_marketing_payback_guide.pdf

Broadbent, S. *The Advertising Budget: Advertiser's guide to budget determination.* McGraw-Hill, 1989

Cook, L and Holmes, M. 'Econometrics explained'. IPA, 2004 http://www.ipa.co.uk/document/econometrics-explained#.WsN769TwbX4

'How share of voice wins market share'. IPA, 2009

Jones, JP. 'Ad spending: maintaining market share'. *Harvard Business Review*, January 1990

Wight, R. *The Peacock's Tail and the Reputation Reflex: The neuroscience of art sponsorship.* Engine, 2007

CHAPTER 8

'Do TV ads "wear out"?' Millward Brown Knowledge Point, February 2012, WARC

'Do TV ads work harder as they "'wear in'"?' Millward Brown Knowledge Point, 2007, WARC

Shotton, R. 'The power of honesty in advertising and why your brand should flaunt its flaws'. The Drum, September 2016 http://www.thedrum.com/opinion/2016/09/21/the-power-honesty-advertising-and-why-your-brand-should-flaunt-its-flaws

CHAPTER 9

Binet, L. 'Beyond the click'. WARC Exclusive, MAP 2011 conference

Binet, L. 'Evaluating marketing communications: a guide to best practice'. *Market Leader*, Summer 2005, WARC

Binet, L. 'Fifteen ways not to evaluate your communications'. *Admap*, February 2006, WARC

Binet, L and Field, P. 'The conflict between accountability and effectiveness'. *Admap*, June 2007, WARC

Binet, L and Field, P. 'The pursuit of effectiveness'. *Market Leader*, Winter 2007, WARC

'Briefing an agency: a best practice guide to briefing communications agencies'. IPA, 2013 Downloadable from the IPA website at www.ipa.co.uk

Carter, S, Cook, L and Feldwick, P. 'How valuable

is the Awareness Index?' Winner of Best Paper at MRS Conference 1991. *Admap*, March 1991, WARC

Cook, L and Holmes, M. 'Econometrics explained'. IPA, 2004 http://www.ipa.co.uk/document/econometrics-explained#.WsN769TwbX4

'Evaluation: a best practice guide to evaluating the effectiveness of your campaigns'. IPA, 2009

King, A and Crewe, I. *The Blunders of Our Governments*, Oneworld, 2013

Leslie, I. 'How the Madmen lost the plot'. The *Financial Times*, November 2015

Moeller, L and Landry, E. *The Four Pillars of Profit-Driven Marketing: How to maximize creativity, accountability, and ROI.* McGraw-Hill, 2009

Reeves, R. *Reality in Advertising*. Widener Classics, 2015

'The expert guide to measuring not counting: how to evaluate social media for marketing communications'. IPA, 2015

REFERENCES

We have not attempted to supply the text with full scholarly referencing, but hope the following references are useful. While endeavouring to acknowledge sources, we apologise if we have made any errors or omissions, and would be grateful if notified of any corrections that should be incorporated in any future editions of the book

CHAPTER 1

References

Binet, L. 'The gift that keeps on giving', John Lewis Christmas advertising 2012–2015. IPA Grand Prix 2016, WARC

Carroll, L. *Alice's Adventures in Wonderland*, Wordsworth Classics, 1992

Kent, J. 'Batchelors Supernoodles: leading from the front'. IPA Effectiveness Bronze Award 1998, WARC

Kompella, K. *The Definitive Book of Branding.* Chapter 5 'What it really means to be a challenger in today's world', Adam Morgan. Sage, 2014

Maunder, S, Cook, L, Young, N, Udale, B, Hough, N and Cox, A. 'O2 – the best way to win new customers? Talk to the ones you already have: the story of O2'. IPA Effectiveness Gold Award 2006, WARC

Parkes, L and Binet, L. 'Marmite: please don't spread it thinly'. IPA Effectiveness Silver Award 2002, WARC

Roach, T, Mawdsley, C and Dorsett, J. 'Sainsbury's: how an idea helped make Sainsbury's great again'.

IPA Effectiveness Gold Award 2008, WARC

Sharpe, A and Bamford, J. 'Tesco: how "every little helps" was a great help to Tesco'. IPA Grand Prix 2000, WARC

Article quotes

'A view from Jeremy Bullmore'. *Campaign*, May 2017

Ehrenberg, A. *Repeat Buying: Facts, theory, and applications*, second edition. Charles Griffin, 1988

If You Want Loyalty Buy A Dog is an album by Little Axe, released in 2011 by On-U Sound

CHAPTER 2

References

Binet, L, Carter, S and Harris, T. 'Foster's: tackling men's worries with a "no worries" attitude'. IPA Effectiveness Grand Prix 2014, WARC

Challis, G, Lustig, B, Wood, J, Binet, L and Carter, S. 'Felix: continuity saved the cat'. IPA Effectiveness Silver Award 2006 (also Felix IPA Effectiveness papers in 1996 and 2000)

Kotler, P. *FAQs on Marketing: Answers and advice by the guru of marketing*. Marshall Cavendish, 2005

Sadler, K, Carter, S, Binet, L and Vass, A. 'Marmite – please look after this brand: the launch of Marmite Squeezy'. IPA Effectiveness Bronze Award 2008, WARC

Article quotes

Hector Laing, ex-Chairman Nabisco, cited in Temporal 2001:1

Warren Buffett, 2008 Chairman's letter

CHAPTER 3

References

Barreyat-Baron, M and Barrie, R. 'Cadbury: how a drumming gorilla beat a path back to growth'. IPA Effectiveness paper 2008, WARC

Boszko, H. 'I pick the round: how a new product format and a change in advertising strategy shook up the tea market'. IPA Effectiveness Award 1990, WARC

Carter, S. 'John Webster: a creative legend's lessons for planners'. *Admap*, February 2013, WARC

Carter, S. 'John Webster: timeless lessons for planners'. *Admap*, April 2014, WARC

Carter, S, Moellmann, A, Binet, L and Raucher, G. 'How Philips used emotion to change the perception of electric razors'. *Admap*, November 2009, WARC

Dunbar, R. *How Many Friends Does One Person Need? Dunbar's Number and other evolutionary quirks*. Faber, 2011

Everett, G. 'Comparethemarket.com – where love was the answer'. APG Creative Strategy Silver Award 2009

Glasner, A. 'Walkers: going from good to great'. IPA Effectiveness Gold Award 2012, WARC

Kahneman, D. *Thinking, Fast and Slow*. Penguin, 2012

Sudjic, D and Loveday, D. *Hello My Name is Paul Smith*. Rizzoli, 2013

Watzlawick, P, Bavelas, J and Jackson, D. *Pragmatics of Human Communication: A study of interactional patterns, pathologies and paradoxes*. Norton, 2014

Article quotes

Gordon, W. 'What do consumers do emotionally with advertising?' *Journal of Advertising Research*, March 2006

Ogilvy, D. *Ogilvy on Advertising*. Crown, 1983

Sharp, B and Romaniuk, J. *How Brands Grow Part 2: Emerging markets, services, durables, new and luxury brands*. OUP, 2015

CHAPTER 4

References

Carter, S and Binet, L. 'Getting the long tail wagging again: how Wall's said goodbye to a serious business challenge'. IPA Effectiveness Silver Award 2016

Gladwell, M. *Outliers: The story of success*. Penguin, 2009

Gordon, W. 'The danger of liking'. *Market Leader*, Quarter 2, 2017, WARC

Rossiter, J and Eagleson, G. 'Conclusions from the ARF's copy research validity project'. *Journal of Advertising Research*, May/June 1994

Westling, T 'Male organ and economic growth: does size matter?' Helsinki Center of Economic Research, July 2011

Article quotes

Bernbach, W. *Bill Burnbach said...* DDB publication, 2003

Harford, T. 'Tim Harford's guide to statistics in a misleading age'. *FT Magazine*, February 2018

Orwell, G. 'In front of your nose'. *Tribune*, 22 March 1946

Ricky Gervais, *Daily Telegraph* interview, August 2011

CHAPTER 5

References

Edgerton, D. *The Shock of the Old: Technology and global history since 1900*. Profile, 2008

Grundy, W. 'End Marmite neglect: how planning saved a British institution by creating a national outrage'. APG Creative Strategy Bronze Award 2015

Orwell, G. 'Politics and the English language'. *Horizon*, April 1946

Orwell, G. 'Why I write'. *Gangrel*, Summer 1946

Article quotes

Conan Doyle, A. *The Adventures of Sherlock Holmes*, 'A Scandal in Bohemia'. George Newnes, 1892

Steinbeck, J. *East of Eden*. Penguin Modern Classics, 2017

Wittgenstein, L. *Tractacus Logico-Philosophicus*. Kegan Paul, 1922

Yeats, WB. 'The Second Coming'. *The Dial*, November 1920

CHAPTER 6

References

Binet, L, Carter, S and Harris, T. 'Foster's: tackling men's worries with a "no worries" attitude'. IPA Effectiveness Grand Prix 2014, WARC

Google Trends: https://trends.google.com/trends/

Google Ngram Viewer: https://books.google.com/ngrams

Gossage, H. *The Book of Gossage*. Copy Workshop, 1995

Thinkbox 'TV Nation': https://www.thinkbox.tv/Research/Thinkbox-research/TV-Nation-Ad-Nation

Toffler, A. *Future Shock*. Pan, 1973

Article quotes

Frederick Mosteller as attributed to in Charles Murray's 'How to accuse the other guy of lying with statistics', *Statistical Science*, August 2005

Gibson, W. *The Economist*, December 2003

Hoffman, R ('Advertising's lost generation'). 'Ad Contrarian' blog, October 2016

Hoffman, R ('Demographic cleansing of ad industry'). 'Ad Contrarian' blog, November 2015

Leslie, I. 'How the Madmen lost the plot'. The *Financial Times*, November 2015

Ritson, M. 'I long for the death of marketing clichés'. *Marketing Week*, April 2017

Ritson, M. 'Marketing deconstructed' AANA lecture in Sydney, July 2016

Shakespeare, W. 'Troilus and Cressida'. *The Complete Works of Shakespeare*. Wordsworth Editions, 1996

CHAPTER 7

References

Ambler, T and Hollier, EA. 'The waste in advertising is the part that works'. *Journal of Advertising Research*, December 2004

Butterworth, R, Reid, C and Binet, L. 'How advertising helped VW and its dealers to recover their profitability'. IPA Effectiveness Gold Award 1998

Ehrenberg, A, Barnard, N, Kennedy, R and Bloom, H. 'Brand advertising as creative publicity'. *Journal of Advertising Research*, July 2002, WARC

IPA TouchPoints, 2017

Thompson, C. 'Is the tipping point toast?' *Fast Company*, February 2008 https://www.fastcompany.com/641124/tipping-point-toast

Article quotes

Ambler, T and Hollier, EA. 'The waste in advertising is the part that works'. *Journal of Advertising Research*, December 2004

Binns, C. 'Precision marketing has gone too far'. Campaignlive, September 2016

Hamish Priest as quoted in 'A view from Arif Durrani', *Campaign*, February 2014

Hoffman, R. 'Ad Contrarian' blog, 9 April 2015

Marc Pritchard, *Wall Street Journal* interview, 2016

CHAPTER 8

References

Bernbach, W. *Bill Bernbach said...* DDB publication, 2003

Binet, L, Müllensiefen, D, and Edwards, P. 'The power of music'. *Admap*, October 2013, WARC

Carter, S. 'John Webster: a creative legend's lessons for planners'. *Admap*, February 2013, WARC

Carter, S. 'John Webster: timeless lessons for planners'. *Admap*, April 2014, WARC

Carter, S. 'Knorr Stock Cubes: how thinking "local" helped CPC develop advertising which toppled the brand leader'. IPA Effectiveness Silver Award 1990, WARC

Carter, S and Dias, S. 'Pulling round the red meat market: advertising's effect along the value chain'. IPA Effectiveness Silver Award 1998, WARC

Carter, S, Cook, L and Feldwick, P. 'Barclaycard: put it away Bough!' IPA Effectiveness Gold Award and Charles Channon Award 1996, WARC

Challis, G, Lustig, B, Wood, J, Binet, L and Carter, S. 'Felix: continuity saved the cat'. IPA Effectiveness Silver Award 2006, WARC

Field. P. 'The link between creativity and effectiveness'. Thinkbox and the IPA, June 2011 https://www.thinkbox.tv/Research/Thinkbox-research/The-link-between-creativity-and-effectiveness

Golding, D, Weavers, H and Knight, P. 'John Lewis: making the nation cry... and buy'. IPA Effectiveness Gold and Grand Prix 2012, WARC

Hopkins, C. *Scientific Advertising*, New Line Publishing, 1923

Notley, J, Carter, S, Edmonds, E, Donoghugh, S and Binet, L. 'Cravendale. Cash from cows: how integrated communication built a premium milk brand'. IPA Effectiveness Gold Award and Charles Channon Award 2004, WARC

O'Hanlon, E and Deykin, A. 'Budweiser – frogs, lizards, whassup? Market share that's what'. IPA Effectiveness Silver Award 2002, WARC

Article quotes

Dahl, R. *Charlie and the Great Glass Elevator.* Puffin 2013

Eliot, T.S. *The Four Quartets,* Harcourt, 1943

Great Minds on Music. An interview with Sir John Hegarty on Music in Advertising. The Berlin School of Creative Leadership. *Forbes,* July 2014

Jeremy Bullmore *Campaign* 21 March 1996

Jeremy Bullmore 'On the Campaign couch', December 2006

Ritson, M. 'Burberry has a big brand challenge to replace Christopher Bailey'.

Marketing Week, November 2017

Walt Disney as quoted in Dave Trott's blog 'As well as not instead of', December 2016

Driven Marketing: How to maximize creativity, accountability, and ROI. McGraw-Hill, 2009

Read, C. *Logic: Deductive and Inductive.* G Richards, 1898

CHAPTER 9

References

Ambler, T. 'ROI is dead: now bury it'. *Admap,* September 2004, WARC

Gosling, B. 'The case for Radion Automatic: a new brand in the Lever portfolio'. IPA Effectiveness Silver Award 1990, WARC

Article quotes

AG Lafley, *Harvard Business Review* interview, April 2011

Bruce Cameron, W. *Informal Sociology: A casual introduction to sociological thinking,* Random House, 1963

Carroll, L. *Alice's Adventures in Wonderland,* Wordsworth Classics, 1992

Moeller, L and Landry, E. *The Four Pillars of Profit-*

Notes:

_____

_____

_____

_____

_____

_____

INDEX

Notes:

_____

_____

_____

_____

_____

_____

Notes:

_____

_____

_____

_____

_____

_____

ABOUT THE AUTHORS